614

368

The Metropolitan Museum of Art

Distributed by New York Graphic Society Ltd.,
Greenwich, Connecticut

An exhibition at The Metropolitan Museum of Art   May 10–August 17, 1969

Art of Oceania, Africa, and the Americas from the Museum of Primitive Art

The staff members of The Museum of Primitive Art
who have written material for this catalogue are:
Robert Goldwater, Chairman of the Administrative Committee
Douglas Newton, Curator
Julie Jones, Associate Curator
Tamara Northern, Associate Curator

Design and format by Norman Ives
Color photography by John T. Hill
Black-and-white photography by Charles Uht
(except Eliot Elisofon, 102, 103, 106, 133,
139, 140, 143; John T. Hill, 85, 183, 184,
185, 455, 465; Lisa Little, 564; Peter Moore,
435; John D. Schiff, 90, 91, 93, 95, 96, 97, 98,
100, 123, 125, 127, 128, 135, 136, 137, 138, 142)

Printed in Great Britain at The Curwen Press Ltd.

Library of Congress catalog card number 73-77259

Foreword

Not too many decades ago the art of the Middle Ages was still called primitive, barbaric, crude, and inexpressive. How curious that seems today!

Not too many years ago the arts of the peoples who lived in Africa, the regions of the Pacific, and the ancient Americas were still looked upon by some as ethnological specimens or as images of an interesting but lesser nature wedded too closely to magical practices, fear, and superstition. How very one-sided and harsh those judgments seem today when we confront these works of art of such expressive power, subtlety, and beauty in this fine exhibition, *Art of Oceania, Africa, and the Americas*!

This exhibition of works of art gathered together for The Museum of Primitive Art by Nelson A. Rockefeller, a collector of high perception, rare sensitivity, and great enthusiasm, is an extraordinarily important event for the Metropolitan. It marks the first time in the 99-year history of the Metropolitan that works of art from these civilizations have ever been shown in a major exhibition. Thus, this stunning show constitutes a truly significant moment of coming of age for this Museum, which is in essence a great encyclopedia of man-created achievements. But, even more important, *Art of Oceania, Africa, and the Americas* affords our public a splendid opportunity to see works of art of incomparable quality: sculptures of wood, stone, and terracotta, precious and semiprecious stone, treasures of gold and silver, of superb textiles and wondrous feathers. And the name of the Metropolitan is, after all, quality.

THOMAS P. F. HOVING
Director, The Metropolitan Museum of Art

Preface

The founding of The Museum of Primitive Art twelve years ago was for me both a culmination and a beginning. More than twenty-five years before, I had begun to collect African, Oceanic, and pre-Columbian art. I was irresistibly drawn to these works by their directness, their vitality and their strong sense of style. The small collection inevitably grew larger.

It seemed to me that here were sculptures that had something to say to our own time, whose inner strength and expressiveness had an affinity with the best of twentieth-century art. Here were works of art that should be known to a larger public. The private collection therefore became the founding nucleus of The Museum of Primitive Art.

At the time of its opening, I formulated the Museum's purpose in these words: 'To integrate primitive art into what is already known of the arts of man, to select objects of outstanding beauty and to exhibit them so that they may be enjoyed in the fullest measure.' In all the Museum's activities, it has kept this goal uppermost. But it has also remembered that understanding increases enjoyment. Therefore, the Museum has documented the works it shows, as far as possible, to explain why and how they were made.

Since 1957, the collections of The Museum of Primitive Art have been greatly enlarged by purchase and gift. Only a small fraction of the collection can be shown in the restricted space of our building at 15 West 54th Street in Manhattan. And so it was with the greatest of pleasure that I accepted on behalf of The Museum of Primitive Art the invitation of The Metropolitan Museum, through Director Thomas Hoving, to organize an exhibition in its spacious galleries. I am doubly pleased because this exhibition is a sure sign that the arts of the indigenous cultures of Oceania, Africa, and the Americas are achieving the recognition their beauty deserves.

I am deeply indebted to the Metropolitan Museum's Director, Thomas Hoving, and his staff for their diligent and inspired cooperation with Robert Goldwater, Chairman of the Administrative Committee, and Douglas Newton, Curator, and others of the staff of The Museum of Primitive Art in preparing the exhibition and its catalogue.

I only regret that my son Michael and my friend René d'Harnoncourt cannot be present to share this triumph. Each did much to make this exhibition possible, Michael as a sensitive and dedicated collector of primitive art for the Museum, René for thirty years as colleague and as vice-president of The Museum of Primitive Art from its founding. Each perished tragically. The art endures.

GOVERNOR NELSON A. ROCKEFELLER
President and Founder, The Museum of Primitive Art

Contents

Introduction

The works in this exhibition come from many places and differ in many ways: in their materials and techniques, in the circumstances of their production and use, in their social and symbolic roles, in their craftsmanship, size, appearance, and style. In fact, their differences—geographical, temporal, functional, and esthetic—so much outweigh their similarities, that if one looks at them individually, one doubtless questions how and why they are related.

They all belong, it is true, to one museum, and represent the character and quality of its collections. That they come from The Museum of Primitive Art gives them one kind of coherence, but it does not explain how they should have been brought together in a museum, so to speak, of their own, and given a single label, nor why the arts of Oceania and Africa (and in part those of the Americas) are only now, for the first time, being given a major showing in The Metropolitan Museum of Art.

If these arts have in the past been allotted a special, and in a sense a secluded place, it is not because they have been unfamiliar. Examples of 'primitive art' have been accessible in museums of 'natural history' for many years. The reasons for their separation from the body of world art lie in the story of our own taste, and in the ways in which the related disciplines of anthropology and archeology approached them.

It is only comparatively recently that the primitive arts have been examined primarily as works of art. American artifacts came briefly to Western attention after the Spanish conquest of the New World, as did, later, Oceanic artifacts following the voyages of Captain Cook and his successors. Although occasionally admired for their virtuosity, these objects were largely examined for what they revealed about other aspects of their cultures. Often they were seen only as the obvious evidence of idolatry, and so were destroyed.

The anthropologist of the nineteenth and twentieth centuries had different concerns, but not much more appreciation. Interested in man's rise from simple beginnings, he saw the arts as documenting the evolution and elaboration of skills and techniques. He was thus much interested in their relative sequence (and where possible their absolute chronology) as evidence of the gradual development of material culture (that is, technology and its artifacts) from its primitive origins toward higher forms. He paid little attention, however, to inherent character and quality. Since he viewed the nonliterate cultures to which European expansion had given him access as survivors of an early evolutionary station on the road to civilization (hence the term 'primitive'), he judged their arts in much the same way—as crude attempts toward the later, more refined achievements of the 'higher' cultures, particularly his own.

But art was evidence of more than material culture: As the visible product of ceremony, ritual, and belief, it could also be used to investigate social organization, magical practice, and religious custom. The anthropologist was struck by the way these primitive arts (unlike the arts of his own culture— or so he thought) always seemed to serve some purpose beyond themselves, so that if they were not directly practical (in which case they were called crafts) they were indirectly so, since they were 'used' toward a further end. He was impressed with the fact that they were always 'functional,' and since his own esthetic made much of art's 'uselessness,' he classified them somewhere below true art.

These preoccupations with art as a source of information rather than for its expressive reality had their parallel among the pre-Columbian archeologists. To the art historian archeology implies a primary interest in art, since from the Renaissance on the study of Mediterranean antiquity has been a branch of humanistic learning. Not so the study of New World antiquity, which, beginning about 1850, developed as a scientific discipline. American archeology, therefore, has been allied not to humanistic studies but to anthropology, and so dedicated to the study of primitive culture.

If the compulsions of their disciplines compelled most anthropologists to look through rather than at works of primitive art, this tendency was reinforced by their own esthetic preferences. These were, quite naturally, conservative, as befitted men of scholarly interests and university connections. With outstanding exceptions their bias was toward a tradition of classicizing naturalism that judged artistic skill upon its ability to reproduce the appearance of nature, and largely forgot that what it accepted as the simulacrum of that appearance was in reality the convention of a single artistic tradition (a convention often breached even in Western art). They might admire the firm skills that controlled the forms of an arbitrary stylization, using them to establish a hierarchy of achievement, but this is about all.

It is thus not surprising that the first wholehearted admiration for the arts of primitive cultures came from outside the academy. The so-called 'discovery' of African sculpture about 1905 by Matisse, Picasso, Kirchner, Kandinsky, and their colleagues was later extended by other artists to encompass the very different qualities of Oceanic and pre-Columbian art. Their view was subjective, highly partial, in a certain sense uninformed. It was based on a romantic, individualistic rebellion against the classicism and naturalism of their own tradition, and they were entirely ignorant of the social and religious contexts that were of primary interest to the anthropologists. This history helps to explain why among the public those interested in modern art were the first to admire primitive art—a link that played a role in the founding and development of The Museum of Primitive Art.

Primitive art is of course neither anticlassical nor antinaturalistic, being outside the Western tradition that makes these concepts meaningful (even though it has its own kinds and degrees of naturalism), and knowledge of its use and setting is just as essential to its understanding as it is to the arts of any other time and culture. Nevertheless the modern artist made a necessary contribution. By his concentration on the visual constituents—material, texture, structure, color, and composition—and by his sensitivity to the affective impact of the resultant symbolic form, he corrected the informational bias of the scientist and focused attention on the expressive power of the primitive arts. Our present approach to the art of Oceania, Africa, and the Americas— how we look at it, and what we look for in it—results from the fusion and the mutual modification of these formerly separate and conflicting points of view.

What does this change of attitude mean for our understanding of this vast, varied, constantly increasing corpus of the arts? First, perhaps, that the term 'primitive' is no longer really meaningful. Still handy as a short, conventional term of reference, it has been drained of its original content. It is now clear that the 'primitive cultures' are not what they were once thought to be—the early, arrested stages of a generally uniform social evolution leading to 'higher cultures.' They have had their own long evolution, and although their technologies may be relatively simple, they have developed their own social complications and subtleties, and their own psychological sophistications and nuances. They are different, not only from more industrialized societies, but also in many basic ways from each other, and nowhere more so than in their arts.

It is equally evident that the works they created are not 'primitive,' if this implies material coarseness, poorly controlled craft, or poverty of concept. If certain methods were lacking, those that were known were brought to their own kind of perfection. Though the Polynesians had no metal, their wood carving, produced with blades of shell and bone, is both rich and delicate; the Olmecs lacked the wheel, but their immense stone sculptures have impressive power and detail; the techniques of early Peruvian textiles have never been surpassed; African figure sculpture fuses rhythmic precision and vitality. The list of examples is practically endless and the proof really no longer needed: although a people's techniques may belong to the Stone or Iron Age, this influences but does not finally impair the control and sophistication of their artistic skills. The level of material culture circumscribes the available techniques, but it limits neither the quality of their use, nor the quality of the artistic ends they serve.

Increasing knowledge has changed other long-accepted notions. The first studies of African and Oceanic arts assumed them to be immutable. It was supposed that their cultures having long attained their evolutionary ceiling, had since existed as upon an unending plateau. The arts, being strictly functional reflections of the needs of their societies, had done the same. For each tribe or kingdom there must be a characteristic style, both typical and unchanging; one searched for prototypical works against which to measure all others.

In part, of course, this search reflected the need to arrange a large body of unfamiliar material. This could best be done by differentiating the most easily classifiable descriptive detail. It repeated a method long familiar to Western art history, based on a belief in necessary correspondence between style and cultural context. This would be particularly direct and immediate, it was thought, in a simpler society. In this method a premium is put upon the characteristic, rather than the exceptional object, and it is understandable that the archeologist (as well as the anthropologist), given the task of working out a sequence of cultures on the sole basis of their artifacts, should define those cultures through their most representative examples—those that contained the largest number of typical features.

There was another assumption, curiously shared by artists and scientists alike, despite their different points of view. If art was the direct emanation of a society, the visible concretion of its collective myth, then logically it was also a collective product, somehow created without the determining intervention of any single individual. Artists' names were unknown, and this reinforced the preconception of the 'primitive artist' unthinkingly following the traditions of his ancestors. Though this now appears to be a very romantic concept, it had an understandable appeal. To the artist, burdened by an excess of isolation and individual invention, it explained the coherence, the intensity, the sense of presence he felt in works that could not be measured on the accustomed scale of naturalism and stylization. To the scientist it seemed the obvious accompaniment of a functionalism he associated more with craft than with creativity. Besides, it was difficult to make distinctions within styles so different from those he knew.

As we have learned more about the arts of Oceania, Africa, and the Americas, we have been forced to revise these assumptions. The history of African and Oceanic art is difficult to establish. There are no written records, and oral traditions, although they are quite accurate in certain societies with a special interest in genealogy, can be accepted only with caution. Traveler's accounts, useful when they exist (as for certain parts of Africa), are few, and rarely precise in their mention of the arts. Occasionally a collector's date can be established, as with those South Seas works traceable to specific voyages—from those of Cook on. Scientific methods of dating are increasingly helpful, and African and Oceanic archeology reinforce the evidence that there has been considerable artistic change. In the end it is the objects themselves that tell us the most. The more we study them, the more their stylistic differences become apparent, differences sometimes due to the coexistence of local traditions but also clearly due to historical alteration.

Since the position of the artist differs from culture to culture, and from tribe to tribe, it is difficult to generalize about his role, though it can be said that he most often is not exclusively an artist but is also an ordinary economic citizen. But both field work and the close study of objects now make it evident that among many peoples his work is not entirely traditional and he is not altogether anonymous. The demands of function limit the range of iconographic and stylistic innovation. But in their own societies, where their ritual significance subjects them to careful scrutiny, and where at best only neighboring styles are known, distinctions invisible to the outsider are easily perceived. Thus both the Asmat and the Abelam of New Guinea distinguish the styles of different villages, and the work of particular artists. The same is true among the Yoruba of Nigeria and elsewhere in Africa. Awareness of this kind generally carries with it judgment of another sort: the judgment of quality. Outstanding artistic ability is recognized, the name of the exceptional artist is known even beyond his own immediate community, and may be remembered for several generations. (Limited as we are to archeological information, we can only infer that the same was probably true in pre-Columbian America.)

What, however, is the nature and basis of this appreciation? These arts are after all mainly functional, and in their most important manifestations entirely so. They cannot be vehicles for the sort of personal expression so important to our own romantic heritage, still less for protest against traditional values. Certainly skill in the handling of tools and materials, in the inclusion and disposition of accepted motifs, is valued by artists and public alike; but does this mean that appreciation is reduced to artisanship and decoration, that is, to those unessential elements that fall outside the realm of function and meaning? Is this all that is left to the esthetic sense?

To pose the question in this fashion—as it has often been posed in the past—is probably to put it wrongly, for it implicitly accepts a separation between the esthetic and the functional aspects of the work of art, and it assumes that art is merely the later illustration of ideas and concepts first elaborated elsewhere. But masks (which, we must remember, were part of a total costume, seen in motion) and figures do not simply narrate an iconography of details. They do not so much represent as embody the powers and spirits they body forth; they shape at least as much as they follow the traditional imagination of an audience that then visualizes in the very concrete formal and expressive terms of the works themselves, which to them seem natural. All aspects of a work are thus essential to its effects, and in nonliterate societies especially, there is finally no way of separating the esthetic from the functional.

What does this mean for our understanding and appreciation? For the arts of 'civilization' we have long accepted both esthetic and cultural relativism. We know that art has many backgrounds and uses, and employs many styles. We know that a broad understanding of the cultural matrix out of which it comes can correct our own subjective view and help us judge it in its own terms and on its own merits, and that this is the first step toward informed enjoyment. The same is true for the arts of 'primitive cultures,' but since the social and religious attitudes of their original setting are much less familiar, the required understanding is harder to come by. To put any of the world's art in a museum is to take it out of its intended environment. But whatever its style, and whatever its cultural source, it possesses certain inherent qualities that render it still accessible. These are the qualities of skill, of design, of expressive form and concentrated emotion that make it *art*. In large measure these qualities can cross cultural boundaries—as much so in the arts of Oceania, Africa, and the Americas as in any other art.

ROBERT GOLDWATER
Chairman of the Administrative Committee,
The Museum of Primitive Art

639

199

Oceania

Many clusters of islands fan out from the coast of Asia into the Pacific Ocean. Those nearest the Indonesian archipelago are of great size: New Guinea, New Zealand, and the continent-sized Australia. Eastward, the islands decrease in size and the groups become more widely separated. Apart from Australia, geographers divide them into three areas: that just north and east of Australia is Melanesia, with Micronesia north of it; Polynesia extends further east.

In spite of the vast expanses of ocean between them, these islands have been inhabited for a very long time. Attempts to trace the early history of Oceania have so far been extremely speculative, based as they are on the evidence of tradition, physical anthropology, linguistics, and the implications of Asian archeology. Recent archeological work in Polynesia and Melanesia, though still sporadic, has necessitated important revisions of theories about dating and distribution; thus, statements about Oceanic history must be, in a sense, more provisional now than before.

The original homes of the Oceanic populations are not definitely known, but almost certainly their paths brought them through southeast Asia in successive migrations. The earliest immigrants were the ancestors of the Australian aborigines. They must have traveled largely on foot across land bridges that have since subsided under the sea; the continent was inhabited by these nomads at least twenty thousand years ago. Further migrations populated New Guinea with people of a different ethnic type with Negroid traits, the Papuans. New archeological evidence from the New Guinea highlands shows that they were already inhabited eleven thousand years ago by groups who were also probably nomadic hunters, and that the technical equipment for extensive agricultural operations which could have supported large populations was in use by New Guinea highlanders at least twenty-five hundred years ago. Parts of Micronesia were colonized before 2000 B.C., probably from the Philippines. Further migrations of dark-skinned peoples followed, causing modifications of the pre-

ceding cultures, and leading to the occupation of Melanesia. New Caledonia and Fiji, for instance, were inhabited by about 1000 B.C. Later still, a new series of migrations by Mongoloid people from Asia brought a new style into the Pacific. This, at first partly Melanesian in character, began to appear about 500 B.C. in the western part of Polynesia; the settlement of eastern Polynesia possibly began in the Marquesas about 200 B.C. Hawaii was settled in the second century A.D. and Easter Island in the fourth century. New Zealand was occupied in at least two stages: the first about the tenth century, the second about 1350 by the 'Great Fleet' from the Society Islands, from which the modern Maori trace their descent.

During the long intervals following each of these movements the Oceanic cultures, in their relative isolation, developed individual characteristics. Often they abandoned old crafts—pottery in most of Polynesia, for example—or refined others. Local conditions and materials partly governed such changes. In all cases the technology was extremely simple, being based on tools of stone, bone, and animal teeth. Although a few small areas produced nothing in the way of visual art (some highland regions of New Guinea) and others comparatively little (parts of Micronesia), these only throw into more vivid contrast the extraordinary productivity of the others, which is all the more amazing since, during pre-European times, the population of Oceania was probably never more than about nine million.

In much of Oceania the expansion of European influence, from the eighteenth century onward, led immediately to the decay of the cultures. The process was in some cases symbiotic, not merely a function of colonialism: Polynesian conceptions of the religious superiority of technical achievement, and New Guinean fascination with material equipment, made these people eager to abandon their own cultures. The introduction of alcohol, firearms, and new diseases proved as fatal to Melanesians as to the American Indian. Also definitive was the depopulation of Australia and Tasmania by outright murder. Generally speaking, the Oceanic cultures are now at an end, and the area is a province of world civilization.

Polynesia

Although the European discovery of Polynesia began when Alvero de Mendaña, sailing westward from Peru in 1595, encountered the Marquesas Islands, the crucial period began only with Wallis's discovery, in 1767, of Tahiti, in central Polynesia. This was followed by the great voyages of James Cook (1769–70, 1772–75, 1777–79), which resulted in a synthesis of previous and minor geographic knowledge of the islands.

Few other episodes in the history of exploration have had such an impact on the intellectual history of the West. The culture of the Polynesians was profoundly sympathetic in a number of ways to eighteenth-century Europe: among other aspects, their carving was greatly admired for its technical brilliance and elegant taste. The appreciation of Polynesian arts and crafts, accordingly, preceded that of any other primitive civilization's: In 1774, Sir Ashton Lever opened a museum in London devoted to works from the Pacific, and it was considered one of the most remarkable sights of the city.

The view of Polynesia as the home of 'the noble savage,' the 'good child of nature,' was enlarged upon by Rousseau and Diderot; their work formed a picture of innocent charm that persists to this day in the debased terms of the film and the travel brochure. But the reports of nineteenth-century missionaries, stressing such barbarities as human sacrifice, infanticide, and cannibalism, darkened the earlier picture and reduced Polynesian artifacts (quantities of which missionaries destroyed) to consideration as incompetent grotesques. This denigration did not begin to lighten until Gauguin awakened interest in Marquesan and Easter Island art at the very end of the century.

The Polynesian islands share many physical features, including their small size (few are as much as fifty miles across) and their volcanic or reef origins. Their economies were based rather on fishing than agriculture, except in New Zealand, with its wide expanses of land. The Polynesians, furthermore, shared a language and many of the most important elements of culture, including hierarchical societies ranked from royal or chiefly families to slaves, and state religions celebrated on stone-built temple platforms.

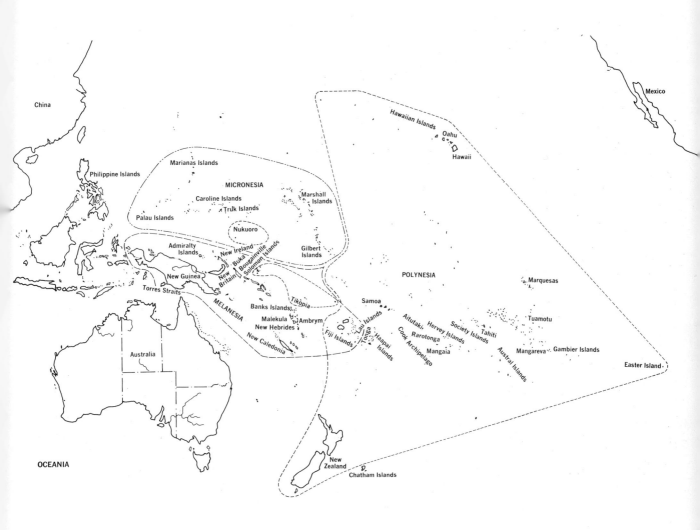

China

Mexico

Philippine Islands

Hawaiian Islands

Oahu

Hawaii

Marianas Islands

MICRONESIA

Caroline Islands

Truk Islands

Marshall Islands

Palau Islands

Nukuoro

Admiralty Islands

New Ireland

Buka

Bougainville

Solomon Islands

Gilbert Islands

POLYNESIA

Marquesas

New Guinea

New Britain

Torres Straits

MELANESIA

Banks Islands

Tikopia

Samoa

Aitutaki

Tuamotu

Malekula

Ambrym

New Hebrides

Lau Islands

Tonga

Hervey Islands

Rarotonga

Society Islands

Tahiti

New Caledonia

Fiji Islands

Haapai Islands

Cook Archipelago

Mangaia

Austral Islands

Mangareva

Gambier Islands

Australia

Easter Island

OCEANIA

New Zealand

Chatham Islands

3

The Polynesians believed in two great spiritual forces, *tabu* and *mana*. *Tabu* was negative, to be avoided, and was determined by priests. *Mana*, supernatural power, pervaded both human beings and material objects. It was inherited from generation to generation; increasing by accretion, it brought priests and chiefs to the point of near divinity. Since it derived partly from excellence and skill, it was an attribute of both the carver (who, as among the Maori, could have priestly status) and his work.

A very high proportion of surviving Polynesian carving consists of elaborate utilitarian objects; figure sculpture is relatively rare. Painting seems to have barely existed beyond overall monochrome coats on some sculpture; color appears as an important element only in the magnificent feather cloaks, helmets, and images of the Hawaiians, printed designs on tapa, and the abstract designs of Maori woven flax cloaks.

Most Polynesian sculpture makes simultaneous use of two nearly antithetic techniques: extremely simplified form and repetitive small-scale geometric surface design. In the basic style of figure sculpture the body is simplified, stocky, with a disproportionately large head. It is found in its most austere form in Fiji and Tonga. A congruous simplicity appears in the bowls and other utensils from the area, but the elaborate clubs from Fiji are often covered with geometric patterns. The figure sculpture of Tahiti is in the same tradition, judging by the meager remains of a style that once encompassed architectural figures of men and animals, towering canoe prows, and other large-scale work. Related to the figures of this area were those of Mangareva in the Tuamotus: divine images in which simplicity only enhances an extraordinary degree of vital naturalism.

In Hawaiian figure carving the planes of the body are emphasized to an almost prismatic degree; the heads, with dramatically contorted features, are often transformed into

ferocious masks. The small figures of Easter Island are even more astonishing, for they include emaciated male ancestors and beings combining lizard and human features. Even here, however, the underlying simplicity of Polynesian art appears in the refined abstraction of the dance paddles (themselves extreme stylizations of the human figure), and in the famous stone colossi on the slopes of the island's central volcano.

Small geometric abstractions from the human head and body are fundamental elements of Cook Islands sculpture; the tendency is carried to an extreme in the Austral Islands, where figures, drums, scoops, and paddles are covered with rows of minute triangular incisions, stars made up of them, and rows of X-shaped forms.

The tendency to surface decoration is even more marked in the Marquesas Islands. The typical human face (possibly owing to Melanesian antecedents) has enormous round eyes; on wood, stone, ivory, and bone figures the head is disproportionately enlarged. Expanded, this face is one of the innumerable units used in allover low relief to decorate other figures, and such objects as bowls and ornaments. The bodies of the Marquesans themselves were the ground for similar total treatment by means of tattooing.

The richest of all Polynesian art areas, both in decorative quality and surviving quantity, is that of the New Zealand Maori. Totally nonnaturalistic in its early, finest phases, its imagery includes wildly stylized human figures (their eyes inlaid with glowing haliotis shell) overlaid with and set against backgrounds of dense scrollwork. Maori wood carving elaborated the architectural members of their great houses, huge canoes, and most weapons, tools, and household equipment. The Maori were equally fine workers in bone and stone (the jade-like nephrite) for weapons and amulets.

1   PENDANT, FEMALE FIGURE
Hawaii
Bone, 2⅜″ high. 61.35

2   FIGURE OF HOUSEHOLD GODDESS
Hawaii
Wood, 12¼″ high. 61.265

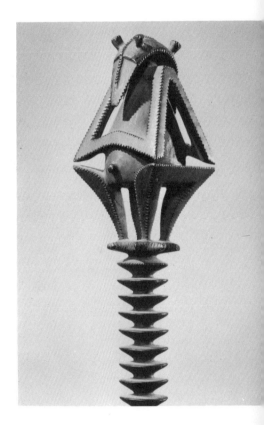

3   STAFF–CLUB
Marquesas Islands
Wood, 60⅛″ long. 57.112

4   HEADDRESS
Marquesas Islands
Tridacna shell, turtle shell, sennit
17⅞″ long. 58.3

5 FAN HANDLE
Marquesas Islands
Wood, 14″ high. 61.79

6 PAIR OF EAR ORNAMENTS
Marquesas Islands
Ivory, 2⅞ and 2¾″ high. 62.30

9 FAN
Marquesas Islands
Ivory, wood, cane, 18½″ high. 66.41

10 DANCE PADDLE
Easter Island
Wood, 32⅞″ high. 56.309

7 FIGURE
Marquesas Islands
Bone, 4⅜″ high. 63.59

8 HEADDRESS
Marquesas Islands
Shell, turtle shell, fiber, 18″ wide. 64.11

11 FEMALE FIGURE
  Easter Island
  Wood, bone, obsidian, 23⅝" high. 57.244

12 MALE FIGURE
  Easter Island
  Wood, bone, obsidian, 17⅞" high. 58.98

13 GORGET
  Easter Island
  Wood, 17¼" long. 59.76

14 MAN–LIZARD FIGURE
  Easter Island
  Wood, bone, obsidian, 20⅛" long. 63.29

26 FIGURE FROM HOUSE POST
Maori, New Zealand
Wood, 43″ high. 58.240

27 MODEL OF WAR CANOE PROW
Maori, New Zealand
Wood, shell inlay, 13¼″ high. 60.63

28 FEATHER BOX
Maori, New Zealand
Wood, shell inlay, 17⅝″ long. 60.126

29 FLUTE
Maori, New Zealand
Wood, cane, 17⅛″ long. 61.77

30 WEAVER'S PEG
Maori, East Cape, New Zealand
Wood, 14⅝″ long. 61.78

31 BIRD SNARE
Maori, New Zealand
Wood, shell inlay, 9¾″ long. 62.72

Micronesia

32 DISH
Matty Islands
Wood, 12⅝″ long. 56.91

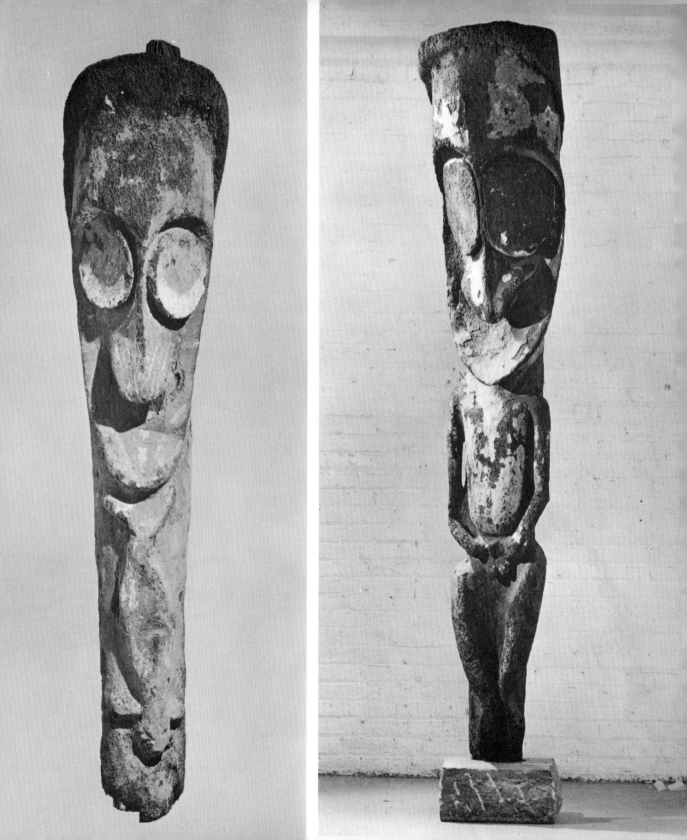

Melanesia

While early Melanesian contacts with Europeans were often disastrous, they were limited in scope. As a result, many elements of the cultures, including religion and the arts, persisted here much longer than in Polynesia. Although some pottery and stone carving was done, the main medium of the artists was wood. Since this is subject to rapid decay in the tropical climate, nearly all the extant Melanesian work dates from no earlier than the late nineteenth century, and most is much more recent.

Melanesian societies were generally classless; men achieved power, which was not hereditary, by force of personality and wealth. Religious life, largely confined to men, centered around special houses in or near which ceremonial activities took place and in which sacred objects were stored. Men entered into religious life by way of initiatory ceremonies at puberty, and participated thereafter in ceremonies that took place at regular intervals. These generally involved cults of ancestors and of spirits embodying natural forces, both of which often included headhunting and cannibalism. In nearly all cases the ceremonies entailed making a wealth of masks, figures, and objects for display. Besides these, houses and household objects were frequently richly decorated with carving and painting. Melanesian artists were quite unawed by the problems of scale; a good deal of their sculpture was of colossal size.

The basic theme of Melanesian art is the human figure, with special emphasis on the head. The figure is often associated with those of animals and birds. Color was used on sculpture and ceramics; the basic palette consisted of red, black, and white. Little painting on flat surfaces—bark or other—was done. A striking aspect was the use of a constructive technique in wood. New Ireland carvers, for instance, built up large figures, or groups of figures, from a number of independently carved pieces. Elsewhere—for example, in the New Hebrides and New Britain—figures were constructed of bark cloth or clay over cane armatures. These had additions of boar tusks, shells, fiber, feathers, flowers, and other materials even more ephemeral than their supports.

The people of the New Hebrides were among the most

productive of Melanesian artists. Here, male society was organized in ascending grades, to which men gained admittance by the sacrifice of pigs; for the ceremonies commemorative figures were made in wood and tree fern. Puppets and masks were also used in these ceremonies, and by hierarchical secret societies. Huge standing slit-gongs, carved with ancestral heads, were beaten for balletic performances which the islanders themselves considered their greatest artistic achievements. All the carvings and masks were brilliantly painted in a wide range of colors.

By contrast, the sculpture of New Caledonia is basically painted black with accents of red. It is largely confined to architectural elements—doorjambs, lintels, sills, and finials of chiefs' houses—all of these incorporating huge human faces in a ferocious, somewhat geometricized style. Masks representing water spirits were made in the same style.

Few masks were made in the Solomon Islands, beyond some of palm spathe, nor was there much large sculpture. Small figures, some for attachment to the prows of war canoes, were painted black, the predominant color in these islands. Figures, clubs, and ceremonial shields were inlaid with shell. Marine shell and turtle shell were also used, here as in New Zealand, to make delicate pectoral ornaments.

The large island of New Britain has several distinct style areas. Masks made of wood were infrequent here except for flat masks with simple features from the offshore Duke of York Islands. Some masks from the Gazelle Peninsula were made from the face bones of human skulls, over-modeled and painted, and the Baining tribes of the interior made masks in bark cloth, painted with geometrical patterns in black, brown, and the artist's own blood. The most remarkable New Britain works are the Baining tribes' slim cylindrical figures, some of them thirty feet high, with enormous heads.

In northwestern New Ireland, a great range of masks and other carvings (collectively called *malanggan*) was made for initiation and funerary festivals, then abandoned to decay when the ceremonies were over. These works are complex: large areas are carved in openwork, with the main figures surrounded by vertical rods or crossing bands. They were always completely covered with finely detailed painting in red, yellow, black, and white.

Sculpture in the Admiralty Islands, largely the work of the Matankol on the coast of Manus Island, was widely traded through the group. Most of it consisted of architectural features, furniture, and especially bowls. Here the human figures, often associated with crocodile heads, were mostly carved in a blocklike convention and painted red, with surface decoration of incised narrow lines of triangular patterns or small crosses in black and white.

New Hebrides

33 GRADE SOCIETY FIGURE
Ambrym Island, New Hebrides
Fernwood, paint, 41¾″ high. 56.242

34 GRADE SOCIETY FIGURE
Probably Ambrym Island, New Hebrides
Fernwood, paint, 80″ high. 57.252

35 GRADE SOCIETY FIGURE
Ambrym Island, New Hebrides
Fernwood, paint, 109″ high. 59.280

36 HEAD FROM SLIT-GONG
Fanla village, Ambrym Island
New Hebrides
Wood, 61¼″ high. 59.281

37 DISH
Ambrym Island, New Hebrides
Wood, 33½″ long. 58.331

40

71

38 MASK
    Malekula Island, New Hebrides
    Clay, bark, cane, paint, 62¼" high. 56.268

39 OVER-MODELED SKULL
    Probably southern Malekula Island
    New Hebrides
    Skull with painted compost, 5¾" high. 58.333

40 HELMET MASK
    Malekula Island, Hew Hebrides
    Wood, straw, compost, paint, tusks, glass
    26" high. 65.103

41 FINIAL HEAD FROM HOUSE
    Big Nambas tribe, Noro village
    Northwest Malekula Island, New Hebrides
    Fernwood, 41" high. 60.107

42 SPEAR SHAFT WITH JUGATED HEADS
    Big Nambas tribe
    Northwest Malekula Island, New Hebrides
    Wood, reed, 19⅛" high. 56.69

43 DISH
    Espiritu Santo Island, New Hebrides
    Wood, 30⅜" long. 68.49

44 GRADE SOCIETY FIGURE
    Banks Islands, New Hebrides
    Fernwood, 54⅜″ high. 59.285

45 GRADE SOCIETY FIGURE
    Banks Islands, New Hebrides
    Fernwood, 104″ high. 56.393

New Caledonia

46 DOOR JAMB
    Northern New Caledonia
    Wood, paint, 76″ high. 66.42

47 DOOR JAMB
    Northern New Caledonia
    Wood, paint, 75½″ high. 66.43

48 FINIAL FIGURE OF HOUSE
    Canala area, New Caledonia
    Wood, paint, 72¾″ high. 56.302

New Britain

49 HEADDRESS
    Chacchat-Baining tribe
    Gazelle Peninsula, New Britain
    Bamboo, barkcloth, paint, 15′ high. 66.45

50 HEADDRESS
    Sulka tribe, New Britain
    Wood, bamboo, fiber, paint, 110″ high. 65.6

51 HEAD
    New Britain
    Stone, 9″ high. 65.125
    Gift of Dr. Marion A. Radcliffe-Taylor

44, 45, 48 | 51

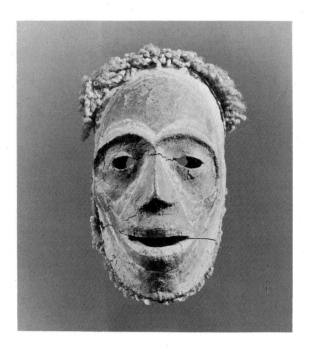

52 MASK
Gunantuna tribe
Gazelle Peninsula, New Britain
Wood, paint, 12$\frac{1}{16}$" high. 67.130

53 MASK
Baining tribe, New Britain
Skull, clay, paint, hair, 9$\frac{7}{8}$" high. 60.155

New Ireland

54 SKULL USED IN RAIN-MAKING MAGIC
New Ireland
Skull, lime, shell, burrs, 7$\frac{3}{4}$" high. 68.45

55 FUNERARY FESTIVAL CARVING
WITH HUMAN HEAD AND FIGURES
New Ireland
Wood, paint, other materials, 97" high. 55.4

56 FUNERARY FESTIVAL CARVING
WITH BIRD AND SNAKE
New Ireland
Wood, paint, other materials, 34" long.
57.205

57 FUNERARY FESTIVAL CARVING
WITH DOUBLE HUMAN FIGURE
New Ireland
Wood, paint, other materials, 42$\frac{7}{8}$" high.
57.90

58 FUNERARY FESTIVAL CARVING
WITH HUMAN FIGURE AND FISH
New Ireland
Wood, paint, other materials, 100$\frac{1}{2}$" high.
56.296

59 FUNERARY FESTIVAL CARVING
WITH BIRDS' AND PIGS' HEADS
New Ireland
Wood, paint, 84½" long. 58.231

60 FUNERARY FESTIVAL CARVING
WITH HUMAN FIGURES
New Ireland
Wood, paint, other materials, 109" long.
66.44

61 MASK
Duke of York Islands, New Ireland
Wood, paint, fiber, 26" high. 67.62

Solomon Islands

62 HELMET MASK
Bougainville Island, Solomon Islands
Barkcloth, paint, wood, bamboo
29¼″ high. 67.108

63 MASK
Nissan Island, Solomon Islands
Barkcloth, paint, wood, bamboo
34⅝″ high. 67.107

64 FUNERARY ORNAMENT
Solomon Islands
Tridacna shell, 6⅞″ wide. 56.82

65 FUNERARY ORNAMENT
Vella Lavella Island, Solomon Islands
Tridacna shell, 7¾″ wide. 56.90

66 FUNERARY ORNAMENT
Choiseul, Solomon Islands
Tridacna shell, 9⅝″ wide. 60.100

67 PECTORAL
Santa Cruz Island, Solomon Islands
Tridacna shell, turtle shell, cord
7⅜″ wide. 58.338

68 PECTORAL
Solomon Islands
Tridacna shell, 2¼″ high. 61.50

69 CEREMONIAL SHIELD
Solomon Islands
Basketry, clay, shell inlay, 33¼″ high. 59.111

70 CANOE PROW FIGURE
New Georgia, Solomon Islands
Wood, shell inlay, 9⅝″ high. 56.86

71 PADDLE
Buka, Solomon Islands
Wood, paint, 67″ long. 66.20

Admiralty Islands

72 PECTORAL
Admiralty Islands
Turtle shell, tridacna shell, 3¼″ wide. 60.49
Gift of Mr. and Mrs. John J. Klejman

73 WAR CHARM
Matankor tribe, Pak Island
Admiralty Islands
Wood, feathers, beads, cloth, paint
16¾″ high. 62.71

74 BOWL
Matankor tribe, Admiralty Islands
Wood, 51″ wide. 56.321

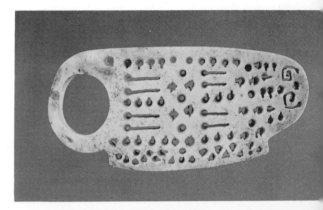

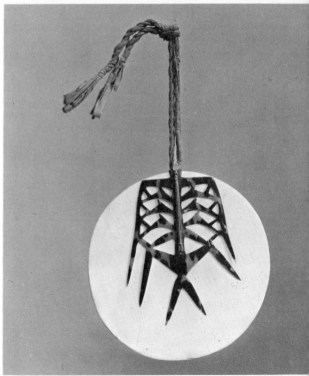

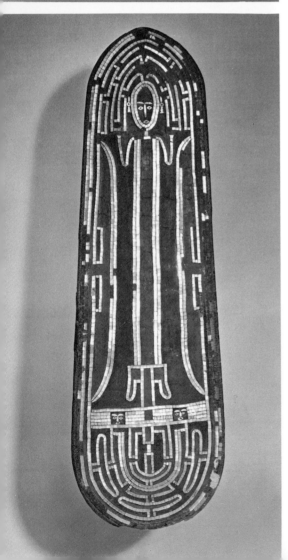

New Guinea

Through the center of New Guinea, an island of over 300,000 square miles, runs a mountain range, falling sharply, north and south, to flat scrub and grassland areas. The New Guineans, numbering fewer than 3,000,000, speak over 700 languages. The people of the highland areas—at least a third of the population—have little visual art beyond fantastic and elaborate personal decoration. The people of the coasts, part of the lowlands, and some of the river areas, have created sculptures and paintings with almost bewildering energy and invention. As elsewhere in Oceania, the indigenous cultures have changed profoundly as the result of contacts with Western civilization. The process has not been uniform. In some cases traditional ways have continued till quite recently, so that the arts, long extinct in some areas, are only now disappearing in others.

Social organization took many forms here, from tiny bands of seminomads in mountain areas to the more common patterns of life in villages, most of which had far fewer than a thousand inhabitants. The most densely peopled areas were in the mountains, where the main food supplies came from the cultivation of sweet potatoes and yams and the raising of pigs. The people of the lowlands tended to cluster along the rivers, with their supplies of fish, and close to swamps, thick with the sago palm, which yields a coarse flour. Everywhere the tribes engaged in intermittent warfare, mainly over land rights, but also because raiding and headhunting were, in many areas, important aspects of religious life. These activities were the principal stimuli for painting, carving, and the arts of music and dance. Masks and figures were the most spectacular cult objects, though the most sacred were often the musical instruments—particularly flutes—the sounds of which were held to be the voices of ancestors or earth and water spirits. The ceremonial houses, cult centers that also functioned as clubhouses for the men, were often huge structures with lavish ornamentation (especially in the Sepik district) including carved posts and finials, and ceilings and gables sheathed in bark paintings.

The great diversity of New Guinea art styles is one result of a complex history of major immigration and constant minor shifts of population with accompanying broken or renewed contacts. Although the historical picture is still vague, waiting upon further archeological work, attempts have been made to trace elements in New Guinea art to sources in the early cultures of Indonesia. It can be said, at least, that both stone-carving and rock-painting traditions of considerable antiquity existed in the central mountains.

A number of major style areas have now been established, and substyles among them are being increasingly recognized. Among the most important is that of the Asmat tribe, along and inland from a sector of the southwest coast. The lofty poles (*bisj*), mounted vertically or diagonally at funerary ceremonies, and depicting ancestors killed in head-hunting raids, are spectacular; hardly less impressive are their immense 'soul ships'—canoes with ancestral figures. The Asmat carved no masks; their masks, instead, were extraordinary creations of netted string.

Along the north coast and the western end of the island, with its offshore archipelagoes, are a number of small style areas. Here are found the openwork canoe prows of Geelvink Bay, least like other New Guinea styles and most associable with the styles of Indonesia. Eastward, at Lake Sentani, are large-scale carvings: great posts and decorative figures from chiefs' houses. The area around the Sepik River is the most prolific of all New Guinea. Along the courses of the river and its tributaries, and along a stretch of the coast as well, there are many styles, ranging from abstraction to a high degree of naturalism. Among the best-known objects are the long-nosed masks of the Iatmul tribe of the middle Sepik, the 'hook' figures and colossal crocodile carvings of the Karawari River, the pottery heads of the Washkuk, and the ancestral figures of the Abelam.

Further east, Astrolabe Bay, with its ancestral figures, and the Huon Gulf, with its bowls and head rests, form two distinct areas. The Massim area, at the eastern tip of New Guinea, is remarkable for the elegance of its small objects, such as spatulas, often produced as trade items.

An area almost as important as the Sepik district was the Gulf of Papua, on the south coast, with its multitude of sacred boards carved in relief and its wealth of bark-cloth masks. From the islands of the Torres Strait, between New Guinea and Australia, come unique masks in turtle shell.

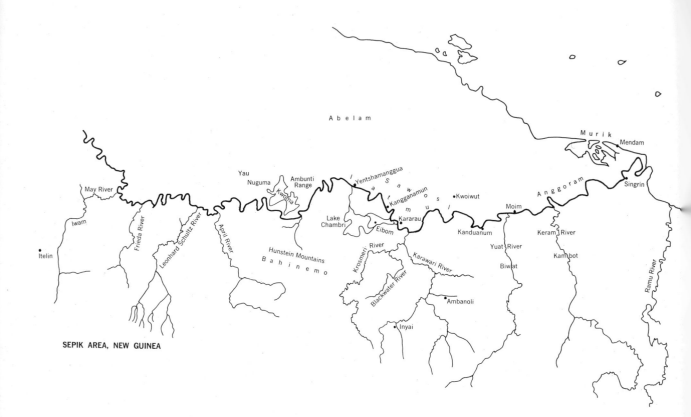

SEPIK AREA, NEW GUINEA

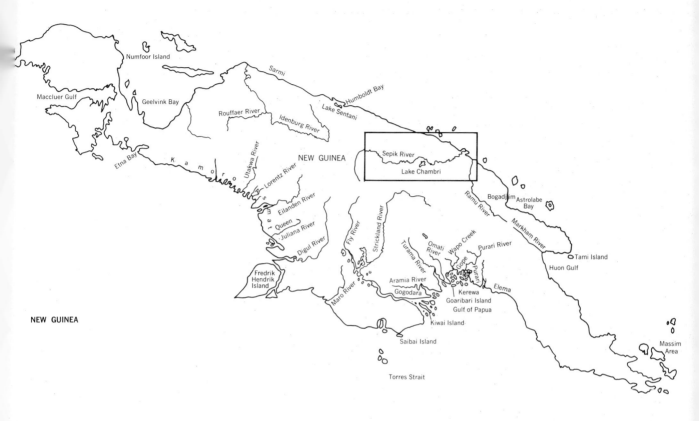

Numfoor Island

Sarmi

Maccluer Gulf

Geelvink Bay

Humboldt Bay

Lake Sentani

Rouffaer River

Idenburg River

NEW GUINEA

Sepik River

Lake Chambri

Etna Bay

K a m o r o

Utakwa River

Lorentz River

Bogadjim

Ramu River

Astrolabe Bay

Eilanden River

Queen

Juliana River

Digul River

Fly River

Strickland River

Turama River

Omati River

Wabo Creek

Gope

Purari River

Markham River

Tami Island

Huon Gulf

Fredrik Hendrik Island

Maro River

Aramia River

Gogodara

Kerewa

Goaribari Island

Gulf of Papua

Elema

Purari

Kiwai Island

NEW GUINEA

Saibai Island

Massim Area

Torres Strait

Coastal Areas

75 LIME SPATULA FOR
    YAM HARVEST CEREMONY
    Tagula Island, Massim area
    Turtle shell, 11¼″ high. 57.87

76 CANOE PROW SPLASHBOARD
    Bwebwaija village, Normanby Island
    Massim area
    Collected by Géza Róheim about 1928
    Wood, paint, 11¼″ high. 61.114
    Gift of Dr. and Mrs. Warner Muensterberger

77 CANOE PROW ORNAMENT
    Murua Island, Massim area
    Wood, paint, 18⅝″ high. 66.26

78 CANOE PROW ORNAMENT
    Suau Island, Massim area
    Wood, paint, 42½″ high. 56.84

79 BOWL
    Tami Island, Huon Gulf
    Wood, lime, 18¼″ long. 67.2

80 HEADREST
    Tami Island, Huon Gulf
    Wood, lime, 4⅞″ high. 59.92

81 MALE FIGURE
    Bogadjim tribe, Astrolabe Bay
    Wood, 37¼″ high. 56.92

77
   81
79

82 MASK
Astrolabe Bay
Wood, 18⅛" high. 58.53

83 DOUBLE FIGURE FROM HOUSE POST
Lake Sentani
Wood, 27¾" high. 56.244

84 MOTHER AND CHILD
Kabiterau village, Lake Sentani
Wood, 36¼" high. 56.225

85 CANOE PROW DECORATION
Sarmi area
Wood, paint, 11½" high. 67.40

86 CANOE PROW DECORATION
Numfoor tribe, Geelvinck Bay
Wood, paint, feathers, 41½" long. 67.43
Gift of Mr. and Mrs. William J.
Strawbridge, Jr.

87 CANOE PROW DECORATION
Numfoor tribe, Geelvinck Bay
Wood, paint, 37½" high. 63.90

185

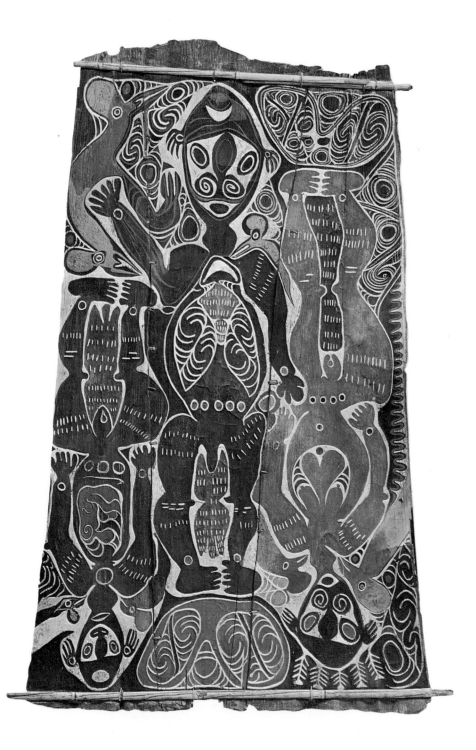

152

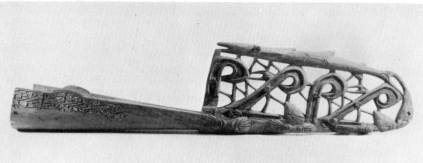

88 CANOE PROW
Asmat tribe, Erma village, Pomatsj River
Carved by Chiskok
Wood, traces of paint, 53″ long. MR 418

89 CANOE PROW
Asmat tribe, Komor village, Undir River
Carved by Amo
Wood, traces of paint, 86″ long. MR 210

90 PADDLE
Asmat tribe, Komor village, Undir River
Carved by Vaman
Wood, 161½″ long. MR 306

91 PADDLE
Asmat tribe, Ewer village, Pek River
Wood, 160″ long. MR 180

92 PADDLE
Asmat tribe, Sjuru village, Asewetsj River
Carved by Chief Warsékomen
Wood, 156¼″ long. MR 174

93 PADDLE
Asmat tribe, Biwar village
Betsj River estuary
Carved by Ambek
Wood, 129″ long. MR 73A

94 PADDLE
Asmat tribe, Biwar village
Betsj River estuary
Carved by Ambek
Wood, 131″ long. MR 73B

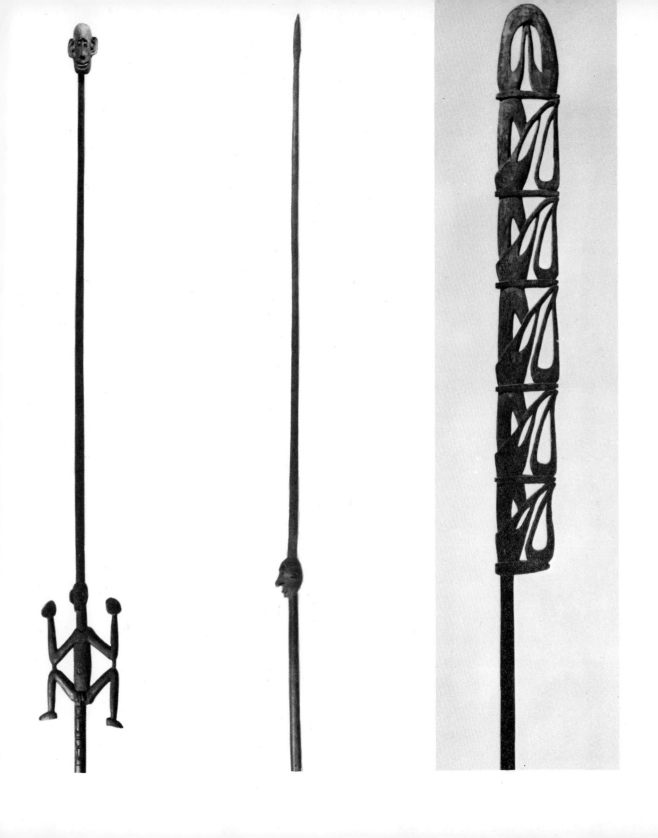

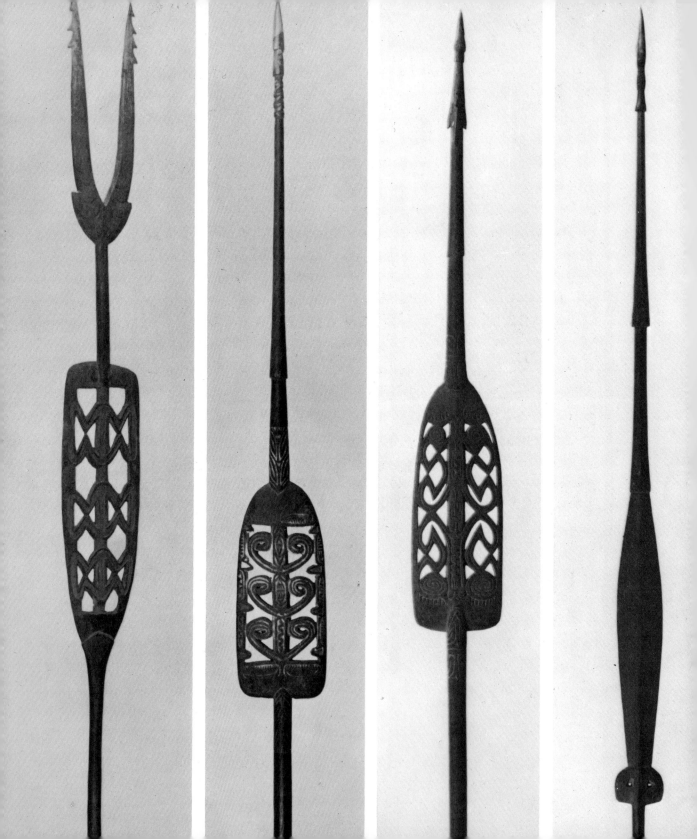

95 SPEAR
Asmat tribe, probably Jufri village
Undir River
Wood, 103″ long. UN 22

96 SPEAR
Asmat tribe, Ewer village, Pek River
Wood, cassowary-claw nail, 109¼″ long
MR 184-1/2

97 SPEAR
Asmat tribe, Per village, on coast between
Asewetsj and Siretsj rivers
Carved by Aurotus
Wood, cassowary-claw nail, 101″ long
MR 121

98 SPEAR
Asmat tribe, Amanamkai village, As River
Carved by Jendu
Wood, cassowary-claw nail, 108″ long
MR 151

99 SPEAR
Asmat tribe, Amanamkai village, As River
Wood, cassowary-claw nail, 109¼″ long
MR 147

100 SPEAR
Asmat tribe, Amanamkai village, As River
Wood, cassowary-claw nail, 106½″ long
MR 145

101 CARVED LOG FOR CEREMONIAL
FOOD CONTAINER
Asmat tribe, Biwar village, Sor River
Wood, paint, fiber, seeds, 87¾″ long
MR 158

95, 96, 97, 98 | 99

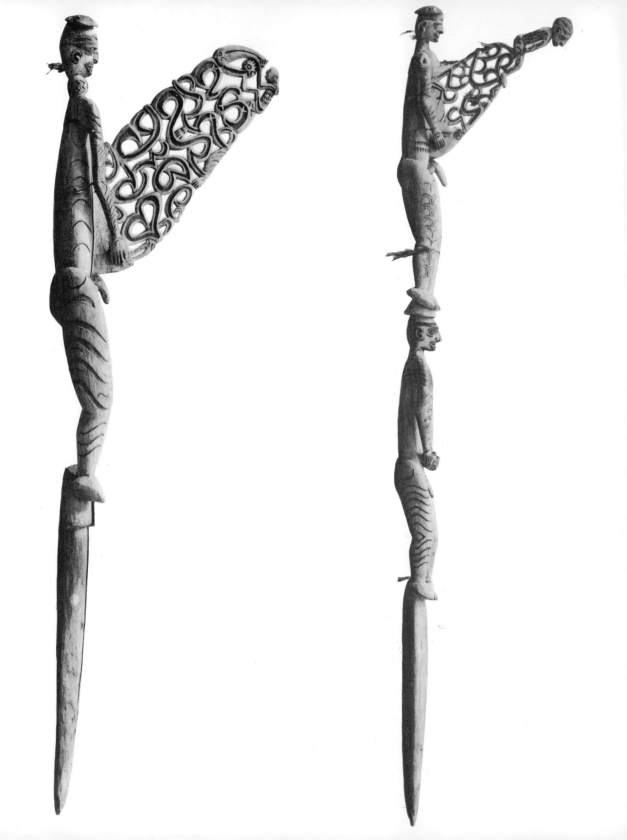

102 CARVED LOG FOR CEREMONIAL
FOOD CONTAINER
Asmat tribe, Biwar village, Sor River
Wood, paint, fiber, seeds, 86½″ long
MR 157

103 CARVED LOG FOR CEREMONIAL
FOOD CONTAINER
Asmat tribe, Betjew village
Upper Utumbuwe River tributary
Carved by Chief Epué
Wood, paint, fiber, 94¼″ long. MR 167

105 ANCESTOR POLE
Asmat tribe, Omadesep village
Faretsj River
Carved by Ajowmien
Wood, paint, fiber, 19′ 1″ high. MR 54

106 ANCESTOR POLE
Asmat tribe, Omadesep village
Faretsj River
Carved by Jewèr
Wood, paint, fiber, 17′ 3″ high. MR 51

104 CARVED LOG FOR CEREMONIAL
FOOD CONTAINER
Asmat tribe, Betjew village
Upper Utumbuwe River tributary
Carved by Chief Cheritepitsj
Wood, paint, fiber, 94″ long. MR 168

107 ANCESTOR POLE
Asmat tribe, Omadesep village
Faretsj River
Carved by Terépos
Wood, paint, fiber, 17′ 11″ high. MR 53

108 ANCESTOR POLE
Asmat tribe, Omadesep village
Faretsj River
Carved by Fanipdas
Wood, paint, fiber, 17′ 9¾″ high. MR 52

109 ANCESTOR POLE
Asmat tribe, probably Per village
on coast between Asewetsj and Siretsj rivers
Wood, paint, 19′ high. UN 5

110 ANCESTOR POLE
Asmat tribe, Otsjanep village, Ewta River
Carved by Chief Bifarq
Wood, paint, fiber, 14′ 3″ high. Otsjanep 2

111 ANCESTOR POLE
Asmat tribe, Otsjanep village, Ewta River
Carved by Jiem
Wood, paint, fiber, 11′ 5½″ high. Otsjanep 3

112 ANCESTOR POLE
Asmat tribe, Otsjanep village, Ewta River
Carved by Jiem
Wood, paint, fiber, 15′ 6″ high. Otsjanep 4

113 ANCESTOR POLE IN FORM OF
CROCODILE
Asmat tribe, Casuarinen Coast
Wood, paint, 111¼″ long. P 280

114 ANCESTOR POLE IN FORM OF
CROCODILE
Asmat tribe, Casuarinen Coast
Wood, paint, 121″ long. P 405

115 ANCESTOR POLE IN FORM OF
CROCODILE
Asmat tribe, Casuarinen Coast
Wood, paint, 80″ long. P 404

116 MASK
Asmat tribe, Pupis village
Upper Pomatsj River tributary
Rattan, sennit, other materials, 76″ high
MR 338A

127, 128 | 132

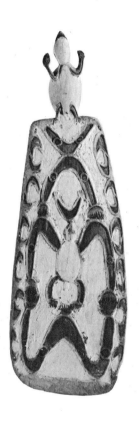

117   MASK
     Asmat tribe, Pupis village
     Upper Pomatsj River tributary
     Rattan, sennit, other materials, 75″ high
     MR 338B

118   MASK
     Asmat tribe, Pupis village
     Upper Pomatsj River tributary
     Rattan, sennit, other materials, 78″ high
     MR 338C

119   MASK
     Asmat tribe, Pupis village
     Upper Pomatsj River tributary
     Rattan, sennit, other materials, 83″ high
     MR 338D

120   MASK
     Asmat tribe, Pupis village(?)
     Upper Pomatsj River tributary
     Rattan, sennit, other materials, 72″ high
     P 365

121 MASK
     Asmat tribe, Pupis village(?)
     Upper Pomatsj River tributary
     Rattan, sennit, other materials, 80″ high
     P 376

122 MASK
     Asmat tribe, Pupis village(?)
     Upper Pomatsj River tributary
     Rattan, sennit, other materials, 80″ high
     P 377

123 MASK
     Asmat tribe, Pupis village(?)
     Upper Pomatsj River tributary
     Rattan, sennit, other materials, 80″ high
     P 375

124 MASK
     Asmat tribe, Momogo village(?)
     Upper Pomatsj River
     Wood, rattan, other materials, 65″ high
     P 356

125 MASK
     Asmat tribe, Biwar village, Sor River
     Made by Jakapit, repainted by Minan
     Rattan, sennit, other materials, 67″ high
     MR 155

126 MASK
     Asmat tribe, Biwar village, Sor River
     Made by Aihaur, repainted by Minan
     Wood, rattan, 65½″ high. MR 156

127 MASK
     Asmat tribe, Ambisu village, Ajip River
     Rattan, other materials, 73″ high. MR 154

133, 135, 136, 137 | 138

128 MASK
  Asmat tribe, Sjuru village, Asewetsj River
  Rattan, other materials, 72″ high. MR 115

129 SHIELD
  Asmat tribe, Sauwa village, Pomatsj River
  Wood, paint, 70″ high. MR 345

130 SHIELD
  Asmat tribe, Erma village, Pomatsj River
  Carved by Pirokus
  Wood, paint, 68″ high. MR 411

131 SHIELD
  Asmat tribe, probably Pupis village
  Upper Pomatsj River tributary
  Wood, paint, 70½″ high. UN 18

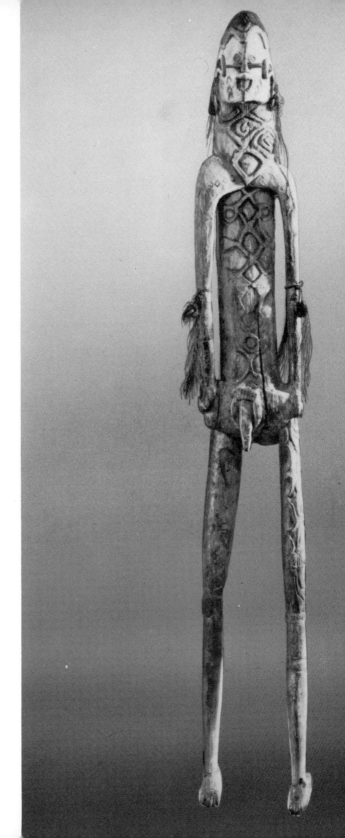

132 SHIELD
   Asmat tribe, Wejo village
   Upper Pomatsj River tributary
   Carved by Jor
   Wood, paint, 74½″ high. MR 334

133 SHIELD
   Asmat tribe, Agani village
   Upper Pomatsj River
   Carved by Posé
   Wood, paint, 58½″ high. MR 406

134 SHIELD
   Asmat tribe, probably Agani village
   Upper Pomatsj River
   Wood, paint, 73½″ high. P 42

135 SHIELD
   Asmat tribe, Monu village
   Upper Undir River
   Wood, paint, 61½″ high. MR 279

136 SHIELD
   Asmat tribe, Monu village
   Upper Undir River
   Carved by Sok
   Wood, paint, 61″ high. MR 274

137 SHIELD
   Asmat tribe, Monu village
   Upper Undir River
   Carved by Aman
   Wood, paint, 71¼″ high. MR 282

138 SHIELD
   Asmat tribe, Tjemor village
   Upper Undir River
   Carved by Mbifan
   Wood, paint, 59½″ high. MR 236

145, 146 | 149

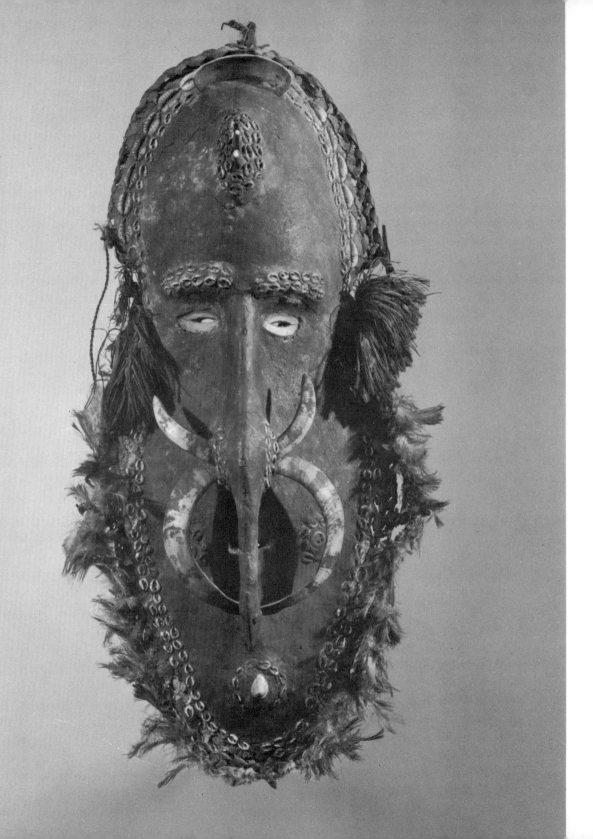

139 SHIELD
Asmat tribe, Betjew village
Upper Utumbuwe River tributary
Wood, paint, 66″ high. MR 170

140 SHIELD
Asmat tribe, Betjew village
Upper Utumbuwe River tributary
Wood, paint, 54″ high. MR 172

141 SHIELD
Asmat tribe, probably Betjew village
Upper Utumbuwe River tributary
Wood, paint, 68″ high. MR 101

142 SHIELD
Asmat tribe, Per village, on coast between
Asewetsj and Siretsj rivers
Wood, paint, 67″ high. MR 126

143 FIGURE
Asmat tribe, Otsjanep village, Ewta River
Wood, paint, fiber, bamboo, 76½″ high
P 401

Sepik District

144 MASK
Anggoram tribe, lower Sepik River
Wood, paint, other materials, 18¾″ high
56.65

145 ANCESTRAL FIGURE
Anggoram tribe, Singrin village
Lower Sepik River
Wood, 71″ high. 58.330

146 ANCESTRAL FIGURE
Anggoram tribe, Singrin village
Lower Sepik River
Collected before 1910
Wood, 77¼″ high. 59.12

147 MALE FIGURE
Anggoram tribe, Moim village
Lower Sepik River
Carved before 1914
Wood, paint, 68″ high. 64.77

148 SHIELD
Anggoram tribe, Kanduanum village
Lower Sepik River
Wood, paint, raffia, 65⅝″ high. 56.269

149 MASK
Anggoram tribe, Kanduanum village
Lower Sepik River
Wood, shell, other materials, 19¾″ high
61.268

150 FIGURE
Anggoram tribe, lower Sepik River
Wood, paint, 30½″ high. 58.79

151 MASK
Kambot tribe, Keram River area
Wood, shell, other materials, 11¼″ high
57.296

152 PAINTING
Kambot tribe, Keram River area
Sago spathe, bamboo, paint, 63¾″ high
56.264

157, 158 | 159

160 DEBATING STOOL
   Western Iatmul tribe
   Middle Sepik River
   Wood, shell, paint, 31″ high. 63.52

161 SKULL
   Iatmul tribe, middle Sepik River
   Skull, paint, other materials, 9¾″ high. 62.41
   Gift of Mr. and Mrs. John J. Klejman

162 DANCE OBJECT
   Western Iatmul tribe
   Yentshamanggua village
   Middle Sepik River
   Wood, paint, other materials, 69″ long. 65.8

163 SHIELD
   Western Iatmul tribe
   Middle Sepik River
   Wood, paint, 54″ high. 56.322

164 MASK
   Western Iatmul tribe
   Middle Sepik River
   Wood, paint, shell, reed, 28⅛″ high. 57.253

165 MASK
Eastern Iatmul tribe
Middle Sepik River
Wood, shell, other materials, 23½″ high
65.44

166 SUSPENSION HOOK
Iatmul tribe, Eibom village
Middle Sepik River
Collected 1934–1935 by La Korrigane
expedition
Wood, 40⅞″ high. 61.278

167 PAIR OF SLIT-GONGS
Eastern Iatmul tribe, Kamindimbit village
Middle Sepik River
Wood, 153½ and 131″ long. 68.54–.55

168 PAIR OF PERCUSSION PLANKS
Eastern Iatmul tribe, Kamindimbit village
Middle Sepik River
Wood, 94 and 88¾″ long. 68.56–.57

169 SUSPENSION HOOK
Central Iatmul tribe, Kangganamun village
Middle Sepik River
Wood, 25½″ high. 68.46

170 DANCE COSTUME REPRESENTING
FEMALE ANCESTOR
Iatmul tribe, middle Sepik River
Wood, rattan, other materials, 58″ high
67.70

171 LIME CONTAINER
Eastern Iatmul tribe
Middle Sepik River
Wood, paint, reed, 22¼″ high. 57.5

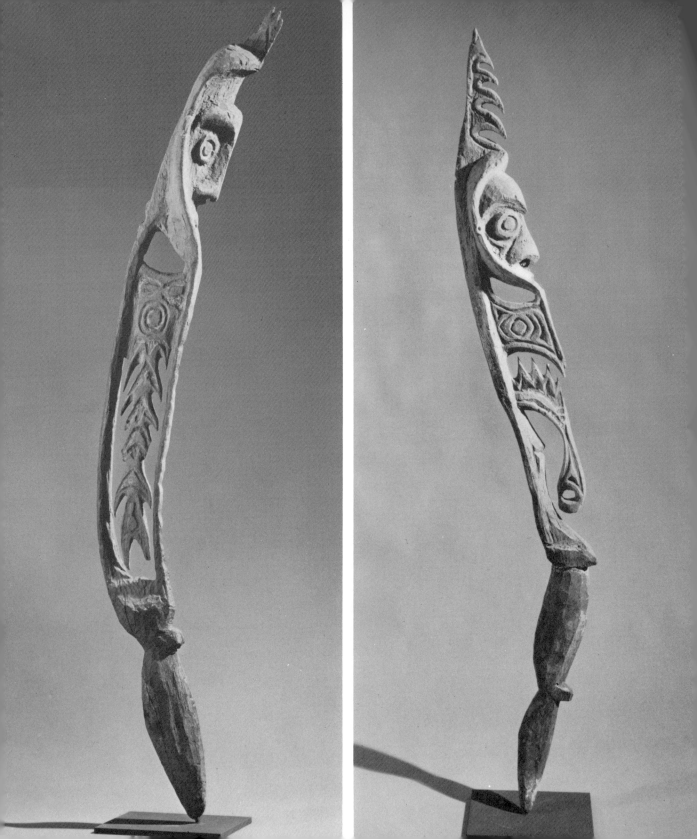

176, 177 | 178

179   FIGURE
Karawari River
Wood, 86″ high. 65.37

180   MALE FIGURE
Karawari River
Wood, paint traces, 18½″ high. 65.79

181   SLIT-GONG LUG
Karawari River
Wood, 35¾″ long. 59.201

182   CROCODILE
Ambanoli village, Karawari River
Wood, paint, 25′ long. 65.16

183 MASK
Blackwater River
Cane, clay, feathers, 22¼" high. 63.8

184 FIGURE
Yaungget tribe, Mburr village
Wood, paint, 54" high. 65.30

185 HEAD
Kwoma tribe, Tongwindjamb village
Ambunti Range
Clay, paint, 15½" high. 65.43

186 VESSEL WITH FACES
Kwoma tribe, Honggwama village
Ambunti Range
Clay, paint, 16" high. 66.48

187 CEREMONIAL HOUSE FACADE
DECORATION, HORNBILL
Northern Abelam tribe
Prince Alexander Mountains
Wood, paint, 44¼" high. 63.7

188 ANCESTRAL FIGURE
Eastern Abelam tribe, probably
Wingei village
Prince Alexander Mountains
Wood, paint, 122" high. 65.65

183
188
186

203 DUGONG-HUNTING CHARM
Kiwai tribe, Fly River
Wood, 24⅜″ long. 61.95

204 CANOE SPLASHBOARD
Kiwai tribe, Fly River
Wood, paint, 32½″ high. 61.64
Gift of Allan Frumkin

205 MASK
Saibai Island, Torres Strait
Wood, paint, string, 19⅞″ high. 56.67

206 MASK
Mabuiag Island, Torres Strait
Turtle shell, other materials, 25″ wide. 67.48

207 MASK
Erub Island, Torres Strait
Turtle shell, hair, 16⅛" high. 59.106

208 RAIN CHARM
Mabuiag Island, Torres Strait
Stone, 5¼" high. 59.211

Australia

Living in a country which is often arid, and a third of which is actual desert, the Australian aborigines remained throughout their history nomadic hunters and food-gatherers. As such, their equipment had to be of the simplest. Clothing of any kind existed only on the south coast, where people used skin cloaks. Shelter, at its most elaborate, consisted of bark lean-tos and windbreaks. The principal materials available were wood and stone; everything made of them had to be easily portable and, if possible, multipurpose. Men had spears, spear-throwers, clubs, boomerangs, and shields; women had wood and bark bowls, baskets, digging sticks, and grinding stones. This list gives no clue to the richness of aboriginal religious and social life. The latter, based on intricate kinship systems and marriage regulations, provided the framework for the operation of the former. Religion, largely concerned with creation and increase, was expressed through a vast body of myth, song, and ritual.

The visual arts, though simple, are of considerable range and often of great sensitivity. Possibly the oldest remaining works—though so far they cannot be dated—are rock engravings, outlined or pecked, usually representing animal and human forms, often in enormous scale. Paintings on the walls and ceilings of rock shelters exist throughout Australia, an ancient art tradition that lasted until recent times. Those of western Arnhem Land, like the paintings made on bark sheets, often use the 'X-ray' style, in which the internal organs of human beings and animals are shown.

Large sculpture appears only in geometric designs engraved on tree trunks in New South Wales, and in huge grave posts and log coffins from Bathurst and the Melville Islands. Most of the small portable equipment is painted and engraved. There are not only a number of different forms of some of the objects, shields and spear-throwers, for in-

stance, but of style areas. Arnhem Land also produces small wooden figures of human beings and animals covered with the fine crosshatch painting typical of the area. Painted shields with abstract designs come from Queensland, and shields painted with snakes or fish from Central Australia. In New South Wales abstract designs, often very delicate, are incised on weapons. Western Australian designs tend to be geometric engravings, covering with subtle textures the surfaces of flat objects such as spear-throwers, shields, and sacred boards.

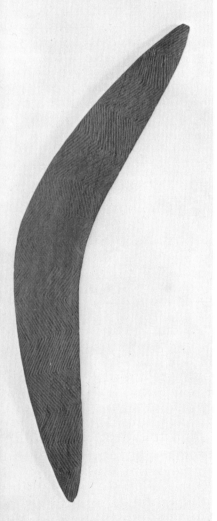

209 PAINTING, TWO KANGAROOS
Oenpelli, Northern Territory
Bark, paint, 40¾×25″. 58.311

210 PUBIC ORNAMENT
Western Australia
Shell, paint, 6½″ high. 60.99

211 PUBIC ORNAMENT
Roebourne, Kimberly area
Western Australia
Shell, hair, paint, 7¼″ high. 59.134

212 BASKET
Queensland
Cane, paint, 21⅜″ high. 61.102

213 SHIELD
Western Australia
Wood, paint, 25″ long. 59.126

214 SHIELD
New South Wales
Wood, paint, 29″ high. 61.120

215 BOOMERANG
Kimberly area, Western Australia
Wood, paint, 21″ long. 61.118

216 SACRED PLAQUE
Pidgentara tribe, Central Australia
Stone, 12″ long. 56.73

217 SACRED BOARD
Central Australia
Wood, paint, 26⅞″ long. 59.128

218 SACRED BOARD
Central Australia
Wood, paint, 29⅝″ long. 59.127

219 SACRED BOARD
Mulga Downs, Western Australia
Wood, 46⅞″ long. 59.129

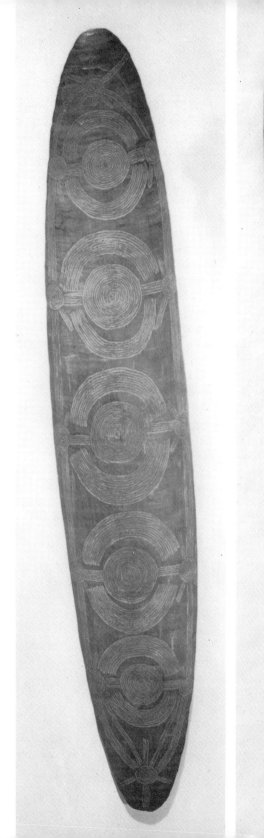

Africa

Various mottoes about Africa that early explorers felt compelled to pronounce still have validity; Herodotus' 'Always something new out of Africa' continues to be applicable to political and social movements on the African continent as it is to its art forms, old and contemporary. The diversity of the continent's morphological-geographical features (it contains some of the world's largest deserts, greatest rivers, and highest mountains) is matched by the many different tribal cultures of agriculturalists, pastoralists, and hunters, who inhabit the continent south of the Sahara and constitute what has come to be known as Black Africa.

It is among the farming communities of the rain forest and adjacent savanna country (such as that along the Guinea Coast and in the Congo Basin) that sculpture—both masks and figures—is made as an important element in the tribal African's daily life and life cycle. Most masks and figures are carved of wood, the artist making use of simple but effective tools. Contrary to the case in other preliterate cultures, iron has been part of the African cultural complex for some two thousand years. The iron-bladed adz roughly fashions the object from the fresh soft wood of a young tree, the knife cuts the finishing touches, and abrasive natural substances, such as leaves and sand, smooth the surface. Figural sculpture is generally monochrome, with a fine dark patina obtained by oils, smoke, and frequent handling. Masks are often polychrome. Before they are used in a ritual they receive a 'redressing'; a fresh application of their colors.

The artists who created these works have remained unknown to us. With a few exceptions it is possible only to establish broad stylistic differentiations within any one tribal area. African sculptors were for the most part also farmers, except in those cultures where the artists working in wood, metal, and leather were organized in guilds under royal patronage. This did not make them anonymous in their own day; a sculptor's fame might be great, and people within a wide radius would commission him to carve a mask or figure. But unlike the artist of a literate society, his signature was his skill and style alone, given expression within the strict limits of the tribal style. His work would gradually be replaced by other variations, when it was not destroyed by the ravages of a climate unsuited to the survival of wood. These same factors account for the difficulty in determining the absolute age of a wood object; by its inflection of the traditional artistic norms it can be assigned a relative age within the slowly evolving tribal style.

African art is primarily religious. As objects of ritual and cult, sculpture contributed in a direct manner to the fulfillment of man's earthly needs. Masks and figures were the embodiment of spirits that could placate natural forces, channel or avoid ill fortune, establish a link with generations before and after, and uphold and reinforce social obligations and values. Their importance thus lay in their function rather than their form.

Incidentally, we must remember that a mask was only one part of a total costume, and that as the dancer bowed and turned (often in the near dark) new and striking aspects of its formal structure were expressively displayed. Music and movement, the missing components when one views a mask today, should be kept in mind.

During the past twenty years our knowledge of African art has increased to the point where works that once had to be described simply as 'West African' or 'Sudanese' can now be assigned to a specific people, and collectors specialize in the variations of a given tribal style or theme. A start has thus been made in establishing a true history of this traditional art, an art which, except in a few areas, is very largely of the past.   T. N.

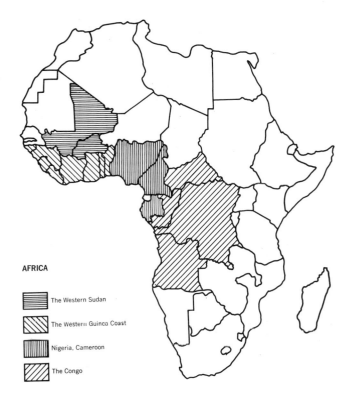

AFRICA

▤ The Western Sudan

▨ The Western Guinea Coast

▥ Nigeria, Cameroon

▧ The Congo

The Western Sudan

The region of the western Sudan extends from the bend of the Niger River in the north to the rain forest belt along the Guinea Coast in the south. This savanna area was once the home of the old Ghana empire and the Gao and Mossi kingdoms. Today its relatively poor land is cultivated by agricultural peoples who live in small village groupings. The Dogon and the Bambara of Mali and the Senufo of the northern Ivory Coast, each totaling some one million souls, are the most numerous. Masks and figure sculpture play an important role in the initiation rites of the men's secret societies, sowing and harvest festivals, and funeral ceremonies. The free-standing sculpture, with few exceptions, represents the human figure. A great many of the masks combine animal and human features. Common to the area is the caste of blacksmiths, who occupy a special place as makers of tools and weapons, and masters of the arts of fire, and who also carve the wooden masks and figures.

Although the various styles of the region (which sometimes influence each other) are clearly recognizable, they share some distinctive characteristics. As a group, these set them off from the styles of the adjacent culture areas. They include a starkness and tautness in the handling of shapes, an accentuation of the vertical in the figures, and a geometric, straight-line treatment of detail. It is also typical that most of these works as we know them have a clean, weathered, light surface (which was in many cases once painted in bright colors), different from the dark, oiled woods of the more southerly regions. The magical human figures of the Senufo and the animal figures and masks of the Bambara, which are covered with the accumulated incrustation of many sacrifices, are an exceptional contrast. Throughout the area there is also iron sculpture of various types.

Dogon sculpture has only really been known in the last decade. Its most mysterious facet is the figures—tightly vertical, often with upraised arms, and heavily encrusted—found in shelters in the Bandiagara cliffs. These works are attributed by the Dogon to an earlier people, the Tellem. Tellem sculpture has been considered simply an early phase of Dogon art, but there are indications that it is indeed a separate style. Predominantly vertical, Dogon figure sculpture is somewhat less compact and rigid. These sometimes hermaphroditic figures contain the kind of multiple reference often found in African art. They are at once mythical heroes of creation, ancestors, and the living symbols of the constructive order of the universe. Kept on family altars, they were rarely seen by outsiders.

Unlike most Sudanese art, Dogon masks were made by the young men who wore them, future initiates into their secret society. Some are human, most are zoomorphic, commemorating the mythic alliance of man with animals, birds, and reptiles. They were used in quantity in the dances that marked the end of the mourning period, when the souls of the deceased were 'encouraged' to leave the world of the living. The Dogon also carve impressive ritual stools and containers, and granary and house doors, all incorporating the human figure with raised arms, said to be praying for rain.

The stylized antelopes of the Bambara are among the best known of all African sculptures. These openwork representations, vertical or horizontal according to the substyle of a given area, were worn as headdresses. Related to the success of the crops, and so to fertility and the water spirit, they danced in pairs at the rites of sowing and the harvest. The Bambara also made a great variety of masks. They functioned in the ceremonies of the six initiation (grade) societies that every Bambara man successively entered as he grew older and learned more of the spiritual and practical knowledge of his people. Only one mask is human, the others again combine animal and human elements, each having a moral significance.

Little is known of the meaning of the many Bambara female figures, although again they are symbolically related to the fertility of nature and the continuity of the people. Angular in style and with considerable variation, they are fuller and more modeled than their Dogon counterparts. The smaller seated or standing figures have long been known, the larger ones, including the impressive maternity groups, only more recently.

Sculpture of many kinds has great importance for Senufo religious ritual and magic. As a result, the blacksmith caste (in which the carver must submit to a special initiation to become more than an artisan) creates an abundance of masks and figures. They are kept in the sacred

THE WESTERN SUDAN

• Locales

grove of the secret society and are essential to initiation and funeral ceremonies and to the agricultural festivals. Senufo masks are composite in character, the animal masks, usually of helmet form, bringing together features drawn from various creatures to produce a symbolically powerful whole, matched by a forceful, blocked-out style. Even the one face mask they carve, small and gracefully carved, is surrounded with imaginative elements.

The Senufo also carve many seated and standing figures of varying sizes. Two types are exceptionally striking: those that, armless and with baluster-like bodies, stand above one type of helmet mask; and the elongated female figures that rise from short legs sunk directly into a heavy round base. The latter invoke the spirits of the earth when they are pounded in a rhythmic dirge during funeral rites. Great colored birds of increase with long beaks and swollen bellies, immense openwork headdresses, and relief doors also attest to the abundance of the Senufo sculptural imagination.

R. G.

220 MASK
Dogon tribe, Mali
Wood, coloring, 60¼″ high. 60.20

221 MASK
Dogon tribe, Mali
Wood, coloring, 43⅝″ high. 61.5

222 MASK
Dogon tribe, Mali
Wood, coloring, 32⅞″ high. 59.288

223 MASK
Dogon tribe, Mali
Wood, coloring, 28¼″ high. 55.8
Gift of René d'Harnoncourt

224 MASK
Dogon tribe, Mali
Wood, coloring, 14⅝″ high. 58.339

225 MASK
Dogon tribe, Mali
Wood, coloring, other materials, 20⅜″ high
56.374

226 MASK
Dogon tribe, Mali
Wood, coloring, 35″ high. 56.363

227 EQUESTRIAN FIGURE
Dogon tribe, Mali
Wood, 27⅛″ high. 58.176

228 STANDING HERMAPHRODITIC FIGURE
Dogon tribe, Mali
Wood, 82⅞″ high. 58.97

229 STANDING FEMALE FIGURE AND CHILD
Dogon tribe, Mali
Wood, 21⅞″ high. 57.222

230 SEATED FEMALE FIGURE
Dogon tribe, Mali
Wood, 22¾″ high. 58.67

231 STANDING FEMALE FIGURE
Tellem tribe, Mali
Wood, 17″ high. 60.18

232 STANDING COUPLE
Tellem tribe, Mali
Wood, 24½″ high. 65.13

233 STANDING FEMALE FIGURE
Tellem tribe, Mali
Wood, 17⅝″ high. 57.221

234 STANDING FEMALE FIGURE
Tellem tribe, Mali
Wood, 11⅜″ high. 58.68

235 STANDING FEMALE FIGURE
SURMOUNTED BY HERMAPHRODITIC
FIGURE
Dogon tribe, Mali
Wood, 29¼″ high. 56.54

236 FEMALE ZOOMORPHIC FIGURE ON STOOL
Dogon tribe, Mali
Wood, 20½″ high. 63.32

237 DOG
Dogon tribe, Mali
Wood, 9¾″ high. 59.284

238 RITUAL COFFER
Dogon tribe, Mali
Wood, 93″ long. 63.91

239 RITUAL OBJECT
Dogon tribe, Mali
Wood, 11″ high. 59.17

240 GRANARY DOOR
Dogon tribe, Mali
Wood, 36½″ high. 58.65

241 HOUSE POST WITH FEMALE FIGURE
Dogon tribe, Mali
Wood, 74¼″ high. 58.328

242 VESSEL WITH LID SURMOUNTED
BY EQUESTRIAN FIGURE
Dogon tribe, Mali
Wood, 33¾″ high. 60.39

243 STANDING FEMALE FIGURE AND CHILD
Dogon or Lobi tribe, Mali or Upper Volta
Wood, 30½″ high. 59.283

244 MASK
Mossi tribe, Upper Volta
Wood, coloring, 30⅜″ high. 58.322

245 MASK
Bobo tribe, Upper Volta
Wood, coloring, 36¼″ high. 58.230

246 MASK
Bobo tribe, Upper Volta
Wood, 28″ high. 61.20

247 MASK
Bambara tribe, Mali
Wood, other materials, 29″ high. 59.286

248 MASK
Bambara tribe, Mali
Wood, cowrie shells, 23⅝″ high. 59.311
Gift of the Carlebach Gallery

249 MASK
Bambara tribe, Marka style, Mali
Wood, brass, 11⅝″ high. 59.186

250 MASK
Bambara tribe, Mali
Wood, seeds, 22¾″ high. 59.309

332

405

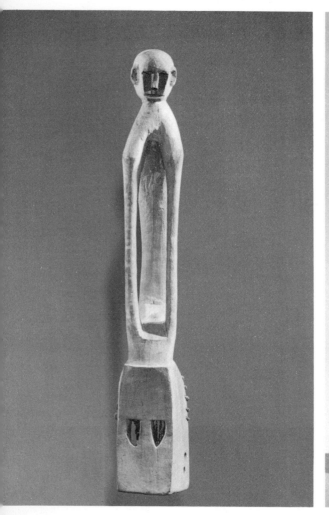

251 HEADPIECE
Bambara tribe, Mali
Cotton cloth, cowrie shells, 11⅜″ high
60.103

252 MASK
Bambara tribe, Mali
Wood, 20¼″ high. 60.5

253 MASK
Bambara tribe, Mali
Wood, 17⅛″ high. 60.3

254 MASK
Bambara tribe, Mali
Wood, 10⅞″ high. 59.290

255 MASK
Bambara tribe, Mali
Wood, other materials, 33¾″ long. 59.301

256 MASK
Malinke tribe, Mali
Wood, 13½″ high. 56.226

257 ANTELOPE HEADPIECE (with basketry cap)
Bambara tribe, Mali
Wood, 22⅝″ high. 59.314

258 ANTELOPE HEADPIECE
Bambara tribe, Mali
Wood, 18¼″ high. 62.37

259 ANTELOPE HEADPIECE
Bambara tribe, Mali
Wood, 27¼″ high. 59.315

260 ANTELOPE HEADPIECE
Bambara tribe, Mali
Wood, 28″ high. 61.249

222, 227 | 228

271   FEMALE HEAD, MARIONETTE
Bambara tribe, Mali
Wood, 8¾″ high. 59.319

272   STANDING FEMALE FIGURE, DOOR LOCK
Bambara tribe, Mali
Wood, 17½″ high. 62.109

273   STAFF WITH FEMALE FIGURE
Bambara tribe, Mali
Iron, 25″ high. 59.308

274   STANDING MALE FIGURE
RHYTHM POUNDER
Senufo tribe, Ivory Coast
Wood, 42½″ high. 58.7

275   STANDING FEMALE FIGURE
Senufo tribe, Ivory Coast
Wood, 34¾″ high. 60.171

276   SEATED FEMALE FIGURE
Senufo tribe, Ivory Coast
Wood, 12½″ high. 66.29

277   STANDING MALE FIGURE
Senufo tribe, Ivory Coast
Wood, 23½″ high. 60.163

278   STANDING FEMALE FIGURE
Senufo, Ivory Coast
Wood, 23⅝″ high. 60.164
Partner to 277

279   STANDING FEMALE FIGURE
Senufo tribe, Ivory Coast
Wood, coloring, 19⅛″ high. 57.234

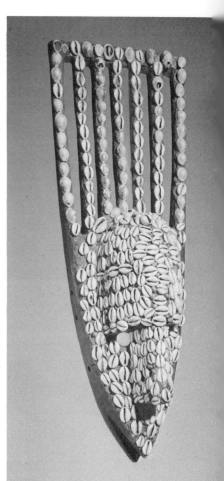

280 STANDING FEMALE FIGURE
Senufo tribe, Ivory Coast
Wood, 10¼″ high. 56.224

281 FIGURE WITH REVOLVING HELMET MASK
Senufo tribe, Ivory Coast
Wood, 12⅝″ high. 59.123

282 FIGURE OF MALEVOLENT FETISH
Senufo tribe, Ivory Coast
Wood, cloth, other materials, 32½″ high
64.3
Gift of Mr. and Mrs. Raymond Wielgus

283 FIGURE OF MALEVOLENT FETISH
Senufo tribe, Ivory Coast
Wood, cloth, other materials, 37¾″ high
59.183

284 FLUTE
Senufo tribe, Ivory Coast
Wood, 36″ high. 62.129

285 BIRD
Senufo tribe, Ivory Coast
Wood, 47¾″ high. 60.60

286 BIRD
Senufo tribe, Ivory Coast
Wood, coloring, 59⅝″ high. 60.57

287 LAMP
Senufo tribe, Ivory Coast
Iron, 47″ high. 65.77

288 HELMET MASK
Senufo tribe, Ivory Coast
Wood, 41¾″ high. 65.78

242, 243, 248 | 252

289 HELMET MASK ('firespitter')
Senufo tribe, Ivory Coast
Wood, 35⅝" long. 57.248

290 DOUBLE HELMET MASK ('firespitter')
Senufo tribe, Ivory Coast
Wood, coloring, 25½" long. 57.266

291 MASK
Senufo tribe, Ivory Coast
Wood, 11⅞" high. 59.6

292 HELMET MASK
Senufo tribe, Ivory Coast
Wood, 27½" high. 56.373

293 HEADDRESS
Senufo tribe, Ivory Coast
Wood, coloring, 50⅝" high. 60.17

294 MASK (in style of 'firespitter')
Senufo tribe, Ivory Coast
Wood, coloring, 34¾" long. 64.13
Gift of Mrs. Gertrud A. Mellon

295 FACE MASK
Senufo tribe, Ivory Coast
Wood, 12½" high. 59.295

296 FACE MASK
Senufo tribe, Ivory Coast
Wood, 15¼" high. 61.183

297 DOUBLE FACE MASK
Senufo tribe, Ivory Coast
Wood, 9¾" high. 60.2

261, 262 | 263

298   FACE MASK
      Senufo tribe, Ivory Coast
      Wood, other materials, 14⅛″ high. 64.10

299   FACE MASK
      Senufo tribe, Ivory Coast
      Wood, 15⅛″ high. 60.169

300   FACE MASK
      Senufo tribe, Ivory Coast
      Wood, 16″ high. 59.293

301   FACE MASK
      Senufo tribe, Ivory Coast
      Wood, 12¼″ high. 56.258

302   FIGURE WITH HUNTING EQUIPMENT
      Senufo or neighboring tribe, Ivory Coast
      Brass, 4″ high. 65.101

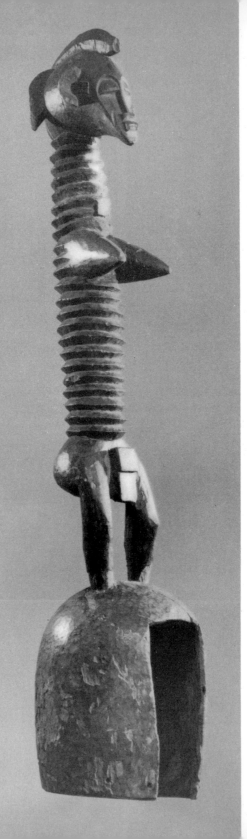

448

428

The Western Guinea Coast

Several culture areas lie within the rain-forest belt called the Guinea Coast, at about the latitude of the equator. In the northwest, within the boundaries of present-day Guinea, the Baga tribe live close to the sea. Their monumental sculpture, including figures, drums, and ritual implements is best illustrated by their *nimba* shoulder masks and sinuously erect polychrome serpents. It centers around the Baga's Simo society, an organization for the cultic promotion of the ubiquitous African principle of increase—fertility of man, beast, and soil.

In the adjacent culture area of Sierra Leone and Liberia stone sculpture—rare in Africa—is found. Human figurines of steatite (*nomoli* and *pomdo*) have been tentatively dated to the sixteenth and seventeenth centuries on the basis of their costume details taken from Portuguese mariners, explorers, and traders of the time. Large heads and figures of another type have been given an equivalent dating. The heads are outstanding among African stone sculpture for their detailed facial features and hair styles. The Mende and Kissi tribes in whose fields these objects have been found claim to have no knowledge of their origin, and their own wood sculpture is very different in style and concept.

Liberia offers a variety of styles, notably those of the Dan and Ngere tribes, which inhabit neighboring territories and share the same culture pattern. Both are known for their wood face masks. The older examples testify to an extraordinary degree of craftsmanship and artistry in their thin surfaces, enhanced by a smooth, dark, translucent patina. The Poro society, which structures the Dan political and religious life, has been considered almost the prototype for West African secret societies. Membership is obligatory; the organization thus reaches into all phases of life. Certain of the Dan masks act as social arbiters by enforcing the tribal values upheld by the Poro.

Further east, in the heart of the Ivory Coast, the Baule tribe offers some of the most delicately executed of African works. Baule masks and figures were among the first to attract the attention of French artists during the first two decades of this century. Baule figures at their best combine a controlled serenity with bold sculptural forms expressed in heavy limbs and a sparse, sexless torso. They are commonly called ancestor figures, but the term is inappropriate if it is taken to mean the portrayal of a specific individual. An African in a tribal society sees himself as a link in the chain of generations that lived before him and that will follow after, both of which require active consideration during his own lifetime. It is thus only in a general sense that the Baule figures might be called ancestral.

The principal people of adjacent Ghana, the former Gold Coast, are the Ashanti. A military federation in the seventeenth century brought great power to the Ashanti, augmented in the following two centuries through extensive trading in gold and slaves with Europeans. Ashanti culture centered around gold; it was found in abundance in the shallow rivers and on the coastal shore, and it gave rise to a lively and witty miniature art of gold and brass objects. Small masks, heads, and animals cast in gold by the lost wax method were emblems used to adorn the king and court notables. Gold dust was the medium of exchange among the Ashanti, and their small storage boxes and measuring weights (known as gold weights) were cast in brass. These objects depict human, animal, and plant life in detail as well as a full roster of inanimate objects used in daily life.

Fairly recent discoveries of terra-cotta funerary sculpture promise to bring to light a new branch of Ashanti art. Ashanti wood sculpture is rare and more or less limited to fertility figures whose main attribute is a large 'moon-shaped' head.

T.N.

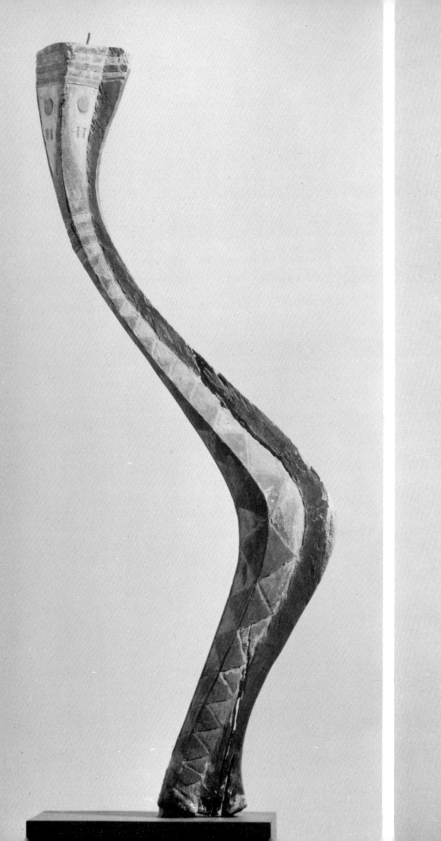

THE WESTERN GUINEA COAST

• Locales

Atlantic Ocean

303   SERPENT
      Baga tribe, Guinea
      Wood, coloring, 68½″ high. 58.335

304   SERPENT
      Baga tribe, Guinea
      Wood, coloring, 54½″ high. 58.336

305   SHOULDER MASK
      Baga tribe, Guinea
      Wood, 46½″ high. 56.261

306   SHOULDER MASK
      Baga tribe, Guinea
      Wood, 30¾″ high. 62.23

307   ANTHROPOMORPHIC FIGURE
      Baga tribe, Guinea
      Wood, 30⅝″ high. 57.268

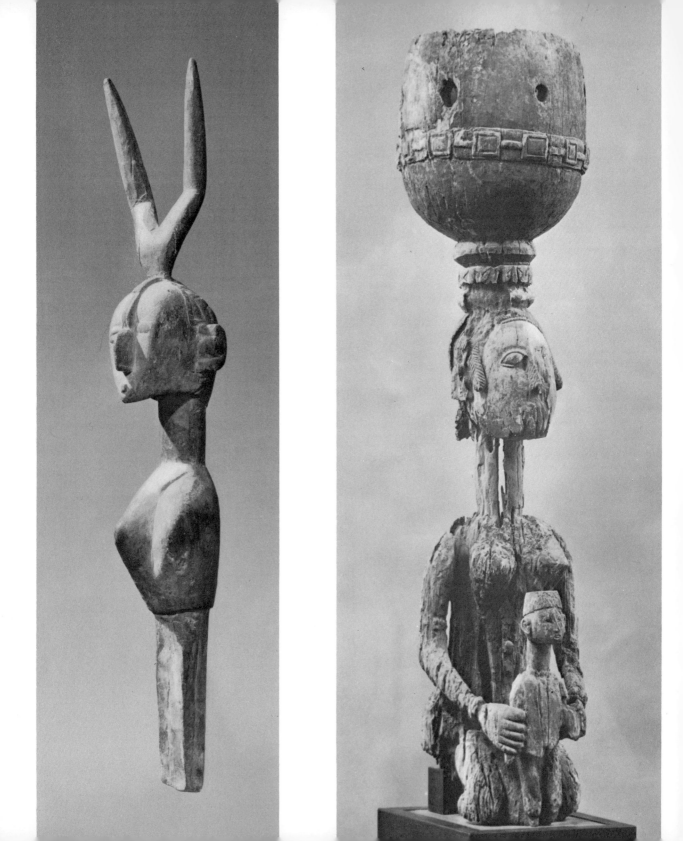

308 SEATED FEMALE FIGURE WITH DRUM
Baga tribe, Guinea
Wood, 39¾" high. 68.72

309 ZOOMORPHIC HEAD
Baga tribe, Guinea
Wood, 23½" high. 57.78

310 MASK
Baga or Landuma tribe, Guinea
Wood, coloring, 52½" high. 57.181

311 MASK
Landuma tribe, Guinea
Wood, 30½" high. 61.76

312 SEATED FEMALE FIGURE
Bijogo tribe, Bissagos Islands
Portuguese Guinea
Wood, coloring, 16" high. 66.60

313 HELMET MASK
Temne tribe, Sierra Leone
Wood, 25" high. 60.129

314 MASK
Toma tribe, Liberia
Wood, 19⅛" high. 58.51

315 HEAD
Guinea, tentatively dated to
16th or 17th century
Steatite, 10¼" high. 60.35

316 SEATED MALE FIGURE
Guinea, tentatively dated to
17th or 18th century
Stone, 19¾" high. 64.31

317 FACE MASK
Dan tribe, Liberia
Wood, 8⅝″ high. 57.109

318 FACE MASK
Dan tribe, Liberia
Wood, other materials, 8⅛″ high. 59.260

319 FACE MASK WITH HELMET
Dan tribe, Liberia
Wood, 12⅜″ high. 63.35

320 CEREMONIAL SPOON
Dan tribe, Liberia
Wood, 23″ high. 63.60

321 FACE MASK
Ngere tribe, Liberia
Wood, other materials, 15″ high. 66.73

322 FACE MASK
Dan or Ngere tribe, Liberia
Wood, 8½″ high. 61.186

323 MASK
Guro tribe, Ivory Coast
Wood, coloring, 18⅜″ high. 58.348

324 STANDING FEMALE FIGURE
Baule tribe, Ivory Coast
Wood, 18⅛″ high. 56.365

325 STANDING MALE FIGURE
Baule tribe, Ivory Coast
Wood, traces of coloring, 21¾″ high. 60.84

326 STANDING FEMALE FIGURE
Baule tribe, Ivory Coast
Wood, traces of coloring, 20⅝″ high. 60.85
Partner to 325

327 STANDING MALE FIGURE
Baule tribe, Ivory Coast
Wood, 16⅝″ high. 56.385

315
316

318, 319, 321

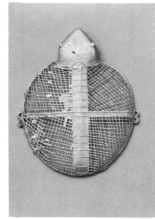

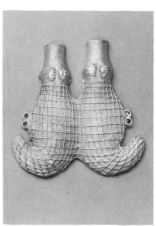

348 OBLONG BOX, GOLD-DUST CONTAINER
Ashanti tribe, Ghana
Brass, 2" high. 60.75

349 CROSS-SHAPED BOX
GOLD-DUST CONTAINER
Ashanti tribe, Ghana
Brass, 1¾" high. 60.78

350 FISH, GOLD WEIGHT
Ashanti tribe, Ghana
Brass, 3¼" high. 68.16

351 BIRD CLAW, GOLD WEIGHT
Ashanti tribe, Ghana
Brass, 3¼" high. 60.79

352 PAIR OF LIONS, ROYAL EMBLEMS
Ashanti tribe, Ghana
Gold, 2¼" high. 61.272–.273

353 EMBLEM IN FORM OF TURTLE
Ashanti tribe, Ghana
Gold, 4" high. 60.36

354 EMBLEM IN FORM OF DOUBLE LIZARD
Ashanti tribe, Ghana
Gold, 3¾" high. 59.303

355 EMBLEM IN FORM OF COILED SNAKE
Ashanti tribe, Ghana
Gold, 1¾" wide. 55.11
Gift of René d'Harnoncourt

356 WATER BUFFALO HEAD
Ewe tribe(?), Togo
Clay, 9" high. 56.36

357 BIRD STAFF
Court of Abomey, Fon tribe, Dahomey
Late 19th century
Brass, copper, tin, 34⅜" high. 58.95

358 SCEPTER
Court of Abomey, Fon tribe, Dahomey
Late 19th century
Silver over wood, 24⅞" high. 57.257

359 ROYAL MEMORIAL STAFF
Court of Abomey, Fon tribe, Dahomey
Late 19th century
Iron, wood, 56½" high. 58.245

360 HEADDRESS, FIGURE OF
SWEET-WATER GODDESS
Yoruba tribe, Dahomey
Wood, coloring, 66" high. 68.70

350
348
352
349
353, 354

Nigeria, Cameroon

Nigeria occupies a special position in the art of Africa. It is the only African region with whose art history—in the sense of a truly evolving chronology of works and styles—we are acquainted. The objects include the earliest dated African sculptures: terra-cotta heads and fragments from Nok, a village in northern Nigeria, which are dated from about 500 B.C. to A.D. 200. On the other hand Nigeria is also *the* African country where sculpture in its traditional form is now still being made and used. One of the largest of African tribes, the Yoruba, numbering about ten million people, inhabit the western part of the country and the eastern and north-central part of adjacent Dahomey. Many Yoruba still worship the traditional deities of an impressive pantheon, each with its own ritual paraphernalia of masks, figures, clothing, and emblems. The most frequent representations are of the thunder god, Shango, characterized by the emblem of a double ax, and the small figures (*ibeji*) that commemorate a dead twin. The number of Yoruba artists working in wood, metal (brass and iron), bead embroidery, and as weavers—not to mention musicians, dancers, and architects—has been and still is enormous.

More than any other African tribe, the Yoruba are an urban people; they are organized in city-states with a ruling priest-king, considered divine, at the head of a hierarchical pyramidal social order. Yoruba culture is heir to the traditions of Ife, an ancient Yoruban city, where the second cornerstone in Nigerian art history, the Ife terra-cotta and brass heads, was discovered between 1910 and 1912 by the German culture historian Leo Frobenius. Of a remarkably sensitive naturalism, these classically proportioned heads, whose striated faces probably indicate the beaded veil protecting the divine king from the gaze of his subjects, were only later recognized to be the antecedents of the brass and bronze art of Benin. Ife's most active artistic phase (the so-called classical period) has been estimated to have lasted about two centuries, somewhere between the mid-tenth and the mid-fifteenth century.

The large body of brass and bronze sculpture from the city-state of Benin has so far offered the only opportunity in all of Africa for systematic art-historical studies. This wealth of works, classified into three periods, has also allowed for the differentiation of substyles and even the recognition of the works of individual artists. According to oral tradition the art of brass casting was introduced to Benin by its neighbor, Ife, in the late thirteenth or early fourteenth century. At the request of the then reigning king of Benin, an artist was sent from Ife to teach the art of casting by the lost wax method; this master is still formally honored by the guild of brass casters in Benin.

The early period of Benin art dates from the fourteenth to the mid-sixteenth century, and the early brass works, such as the tall-capped heads of queen mothers, show a stylistic affinity with Ife. Technically, these heads, as well as the quite prognathous Benin heads with short bead collar and strands of beads adorning the flat cap on either side, are related to Ife in the extraordinary thinness of their casting. Small ivory masks, a king's royal insignia, also date from Benin's early period.

Benin's second or middle period, often called 'classical,' extends from about 1550 to 1680. In 1668 the Dutch traveler Dapper visited Benin; his description of the royal palace, approached by broad avenues lined with houses and courtyards in which rows of wood pillars displayed bronze plaques, accounts for much of our historical knowledge of Benin. These plaques, which have survived in quantity, form the single most detailed source of information about life at the court of Benin. Other sculptures of the middle period include heads with high bead collars, used as tusk holders for royal ancestor shrines, and free-standing figures.

Benin's third period extends from about 1700 to 1897. A temporary collapse of the empire in the early eighteenth century is perhaps reflected in the waning quality of the craft and style of its later bronze works. But there are certain types of objects, such as the leopards and free-standing royal figures, which in their splendor equal the earlier objects.

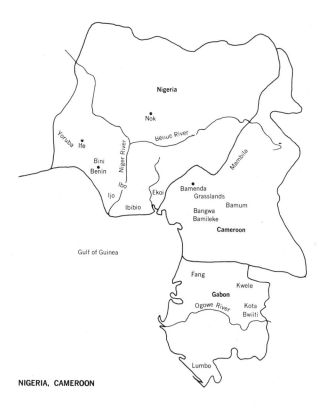

NIGERIA, CAMEROON

The formalization of court life was mirrored in the hieratic art of Benin, created by guild artists who worked and moved within the established canons of taste under royal patronage. Certain phases of their production have been deplored for their empty formalism and lack of the vitality found in peasant religious art, but the art as a whole must still be granted its absolute mastery of medium and its formal magnificence.

The tribal art of northern Nigeria (the Afo, Tiv, Chamba, and Mambila tribes) and that of the important Niger delta and Cross River tribes in the southeast extends into Cameroon, which adjoins Nigeria at its eastern border. Although the Cameroon grasslands have had a prolific artistic production in wood, brass, clay, and bead embroidery, this art is at present probably the least familiar of all African arts. The political structure of the grassland tribes (Kom, Nsaw, Bamum, Bangwa, Bamileke) is that of small independent states within the larger context of a fairly homogeneous culture area. Accordingly, much of Cameroon art has focused around the person of the king, the divine ruler. Royal ancestor and effigy figures, portals with high-relief sculpture, carved and beaded thrones and vessels, drinking horns, brass and clay pipes, and oliphants have been created by guild artists as ceremonial symbols of the ruler's authority. The royal ancestor figures of the Bangwa and Bamileke are outstanding among African figural sculpture for their dynamic and dramatic poses, and expressions of radiant vitality. In sharp contrast are the figures of the Kom, whose placid serenity is heightened by a rigidly static pose; these figures are frequently totally covered with red, black, and blue glass beads.

From Gabon, the coastal republic between Cameroon and the Congo, come the much-admired Fang reliquary figures and heart-shaped, often white-faced masks. The Fang, as well as the neighboring Kota, retain some bodily remains of their deceased in baskets, upon which the guardian or reliquary figure is placed.

T. N.

Ever since the disclosure of these treasures by the British punitive expedition to Benin in 1897, there has been considerable speculation as to the origin of African brass and bronze casting. At first Mediterranean or Egyptian influences were postulated; at present it is widely believed that it is indigenous to Black Africa, though the origin of the component parts of the alloys remains problematic.

Court art by its very nature differs from the religious sculpture of African farming communities; it serves the state by proclaiming its prosperity and endurance, furnishing liturgical objects for the religious cults, and royal and aristocratic insignia as symbols of power. In Benin, as in other African states, the king was considered to rule by divine right. He was the vessel through which divine forces were made available to his subjects. In his person he thus ensured the state's well-being.

361   PLAQUE WITH ROYAL DIGNITARY
Court of Benin, Bini tribe, Nigeria
About 1550–1680
Bronze, 15¾″ high. 58.70

362   PLAQUE WITH SERPENT
Court of Benin, Bini tribe, Nigeria
About 1550–1680
Bronze, 18½″ high. 58.254

363   PLAQUE WITH WARRIOR
Court of Benin, Bini tribe, Nigeria
About 1550–1680
Bronze, 18⅝″ high. 58.256

364   PLAQUE WITH KING
Court of Benin, Bini tribe, Nigeria
About 1550–1680
Bronze, 16½″ high. 62.171
Gift of Samuel Rubin

365   PLAQUE WITH KING AND ATTENDANTS
Court of Benin, Bini tribe, Nigeria
About 1550–1680
Bronze, 19½″ high. 57.231

366   PLAQUE WITH WARRIOR
Court of Benin, Bini tribe, Nigeria
About 1550–1680
Bronze, 18″ high. 58.255

367   HEAD
Court of Benin, Bini tribe, Nigeria
About 1550–1680
Bronze, 10¾″ high. 58.218

368   HEAD
Court of Benin, Bini tribe, Nigeria
About 1550
Bronze, 9¼″ high. 58.181

369 HEAD
Court of Benin, Bini tribe, Nigeria
About 1550
Bronze, 8⅜″ high. 58.180

370 BELT MASK
Court of Benin, Bini tribe, Nigeria
Shortly after 1550
Ivory, 9⅜″ high. 58.100

371 ALTAR STAND
Court of Benin, Bini tribe, Nigeria
19th century
Bronze, 10⅛″ high. 61.185

372 STAFF WITH IBIS, IDIOPHONE
Court of Benin, Bini tribe, Nigeria
Early 19th century
Bronze, 14″ high. 56.338

373 HEAD OF A RAM
Lower Niger Valley, Nigeria
About 1750
Bronze, 7½″ high. 58.219

374 LEOPARD
Court of Benin, Bini tribe, Nigeria
About 1750
Bronze, 15½″ high. 58.90

375 LEOPARD HEAD
Court of Benin, Bini tribe, Nigeria
17th century
Bronze, 8⅝″ high. 57.118

376 STANDING FIGURE OF HORN-BLOWER
Court of Benin, Bini tribe, Nigeria
About 1550–1680
Bronze, 24⅞″ high. 57.255

370, 373 | 374
375

377 BRACELET
Court of Benin, Bini tribe, Nigeria
17th or 18th century
Ivory, 4″ high. 56.352

378 BRACELET
Court of Benin, Bini tribe, Nigeria
17th or 18th century
Ivory, copper, 5⅛″ high. 58.341

379 STANDING FEMALE FIGURE
Court of Benin, Bini tribe, Nigeria
About 1800
Ivory, 13″ high. 57.80

380 CARVED TUSK
Court of Benin, Bini tribe, Nigeria
19th century
Ivory, 74″ high. 63.166

381 HEAD
Town of Esie, Ilorin province, Nigeria
Soapstone, 11¾″ high. 66.30

382 STANDING MOTHER AND CHILD FIGURE
Yoruba tribe, Nigeria
Wood, coloring, 28½″ high. 56.220

383 MASK
Yoruba tribe, Nigeria
Wood, coloring, 16″ high. 60.145

384 HEADDRESS
Yoruba tribe, Nigeria
Wood, coloring, 10⅞″ high. 60.86

385 STANDING MALE TWIN FIGURE
WITH COAT
Yoruba tribe, Nigeria
Wood, cotton cloth, cowrie shells, 12″ high
61.68

386 STAFF
Yoruba tribe, Nigeria
Bronze, 7¼″ high. 59.296

387 MASK
Ibibio tribe, Nigeria
Wood, coloring, 22⅜″ high. 59.32

388 MASK
Ibibio tribe, Nigeria
Wood, 23″ high. 55.5
Gift of Mrs. Margaret Plass

389 MASK
Ibo tribe, Nigeria
Wood, 19″ high. 66.50

406 SEATED MALE FIGURE FOR RELIQUARY
Fang tribe, Gabon
Wood, 27″ high. 66.39
Gift of IBM Corporation

407 FIGURE FOR RELIQUARY
Shake or neighboring tribe, Gabon
Wood, copper, brass, 20⅜″ high. 61.247

408 FIGURE FOR RELIQUARY
Kota tribe, Gabon
Wood, copper, brass, 21½″ high. 57.230

409 FIGURE FOR RELIQUARY
Kota tribe, Gabon
Wood, brass, 16⅝″ high. 59.11

410 MASK
Kwele tribe, Congo-Brazzaville
Wood, coloring, 17¼″ high. 57.236

411 MASK
Kwele tribe, Congo-Brazzaville
Wood, coloring, 20¾″ high. 56.218

412 MASK
Ogowe River area, Gabon
Wood, coloring, 11⅜″ high. 56.403
Gift of Eliot Elisofon

413 STANDING FEMALE FIGURE
Lumbo tribe, Gabon
Wood, coloring, 15⅝″ high. 56.369

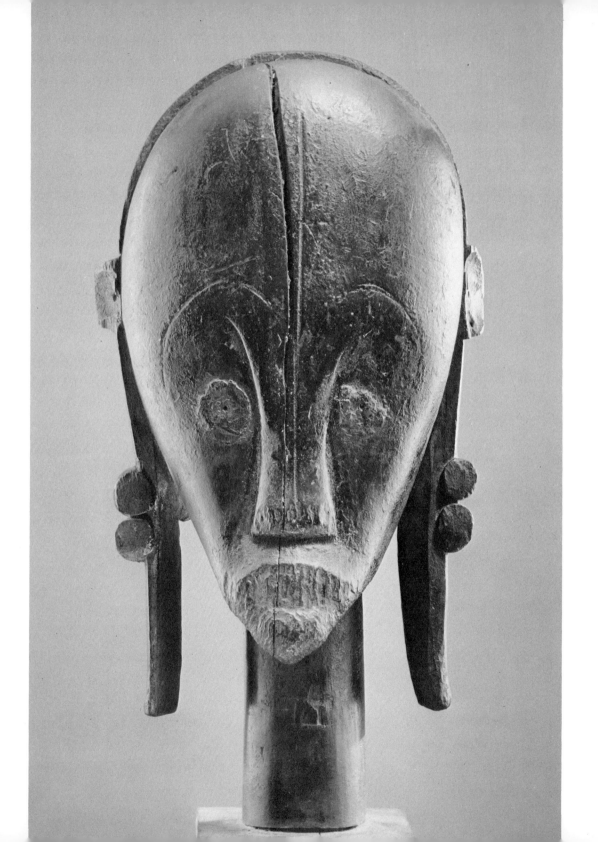

 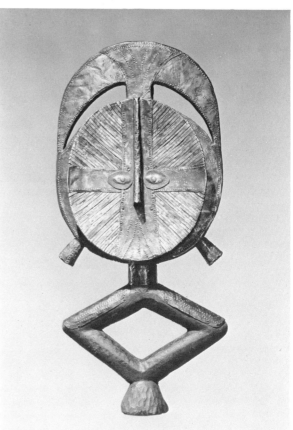

407, 408 | 411, 413

The Congo

The northern half of the vast land mass of Central Africa traversed by the Congo, Kasai, and Ubangi river systems is equatorial rain forest; its southern part is wooded savanna, stretching east from the mouth of the Congo River. Apart from a few nomadic Pygmy groups, the many tribes that inhabit the area practice forest agriculture supplemented by hunting and fishing.

The forest region has produced comparatively little art. Its most characteristic expression is perhaps the masks and the stylized figurines in ivory, bone, or wood of the Lega tribe.

The great wealth of Congo art is found in the savanna belt. Here cultures of considerable homogeneity developed centralized tribal structures ruled by a king. Although these did not always control a large area, they are referred to as empires. From west to east they are the Kongo, Teke, Mbala, Yaka, Pende, Lele, Kuba, Songe, Luba, and Chokwe-Lunda, and these names are synonymous with the main style centers.

Since it functioned in the context of the farming village, Congo art is largely a 'peasant art.' However, the organized structure of the savanna kingdoms fostered the general development of material culture and so helped the arts to flourish. It made possible extensive trading, which in the eighteenth and nineteenth centuries extended from coast to coast, thus enriching the repertory of materials and skills, and it assigned segments of the population to specific occupations, including carving and weaving.

From the village level to that of the paramount chief, the arts served as signs of rank and power. Staffs and scepters indicate the authority of the state; elaborately carved neck rests, stools, cups, pipes, and combs point to the chief's social standing. The female figure that supports the fine stools of the Luba, Songe, and Chokwe is reminiscent of a time when chiefs were carried by slaves. Among the Kongo (inhabitants of the first Central African state the exploring Portuguese encountered in 1482), a family's social standing is also symbolized through the theme of the mother and child. Throughout Central Africa the representation of the female figure is expressive of fecundity and life force and is also perhaps associated with the matri-linear system of descent. Although some well-known Congo works, the Kuba royal effigy figures, are part of a court art, the large body of Kuba carving, which includes masks, animals, cups, and other utensils, functioned in a more general social context. The Kuba also fashion finely worked ceremonial weapons of iron and copper (as do the Songe), and they and the Kongo weave geometrically ornamented raffia pile cloths.

Although each tribe has evolved a characteristic style, Congolese sculpture as a whole has unifying traits of style and function. Masks are often highly stylized or combine unrealistic elements with human and animal features. As is general throughout Africa, they embody supernatural forces on whose performance the all-important ritual life-cycle of birth, puberty, marriage, and death depends. Congolese figure sculpture, on the other hand, is rather naturalistic, with rounded body forms and detailed elaboration of surface decoration. Many of these figures (among the Kongo, Teke, Yaka, and Songe) are considered to be fetishes. Fixed to their bodies are magical substances which, when properly activated, are said to release spirits that exercise their powers of protection or prevention, or else do harm. The so-called nail fetish of the Kongo is only the best known of several different kinds.

T. N.

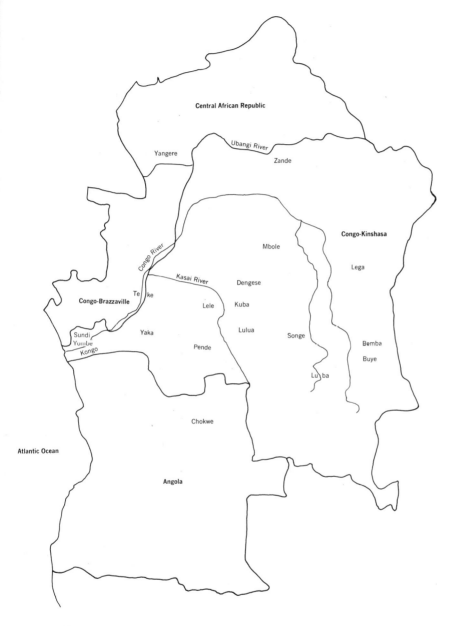

Central African Republic

Yangere

Ubangi River

Zande

Congo River

Mbole

Congo-Kinshasa

Lega

Kasai River

Dengese

Te ke

Congo-Brazzaville

Lele

Kuba

Sundi

Yaka

Lulua

Songe

Bemba

Yombe

Buye

Kongo

Pende

Lu ba

Chokwe

Atlantic Ocean

Angola

CONGO

⌒ Rivers

— Borders of countries

414 STANDING FIGURE
MALEVOLENT FETISH
Sundi tribe, Congo-Kinshasa
Wood, other materials, 11″ high. 65.98

415 KNEELING MALE FIGURE, FETISH
Kongo tribe, Congo-Kinshasa
Wood, other materials, 11¼″ high. 66.33

416 STANDING FIGURE
MALEVOLENT FETISH
Kongo tribe, Congo-Kinshasa
Wood, other materials, 23⅛″ high. 59.154

417 MASK
Kongo tribe, Congo-Kinshasa
Wood, 14⅝″ high. 56.347

418 SEATED FEMALE FIGURE WITH CHILD
Yombe tribe, Congo-Kinshasa
Wood, 13⅝″ high. 56.351

419 STANDING FIGURE, FETISH
Teke tribe, Congo-Brazzaville
Wood, other materials, 11⅛″ high. 65.12

426 | 424
| 427

420 STANDING DOUBLE FIGURE,
MALE AND FEMALE, FETISH
Yaka tribe, Congo-Kinshasa
Wood, coloring, 18⅛″ high. 57.28

421 MASK
Yaka tribe, Congo-Kinshasa
Wood, coloring, other materials, 19″ high
64.34

422 AMULET
Pende tribe, Congo-Kinshasa
Ivory, 2¾″ high. 67.117

423 AMULET
Pende tribe, Congo-Kinshasa
Ivory, 2¾″ high. 68.26

424 STOOL WITH CARYATID
Chokwe tribe, Angola
Wood, brass studs, 9¾″ high. 67.53

425 STAFF SURMOUNTED BY
EQUESTRIAN FIGURE
Chokwe tribe, Angola
Wood, 19⅛″ high. 59.212

426 MASK
Luba tribe, Congo-Kinshasa
Wood, coloring, 14⅝″ high. 56.56

427 FEMALE FIGURE SEATED ON STOOL
Luba tribe, Congo-Kinshasa
Wood, 9″ high. 57.26

428 FEMALE HALF FIGURE, FETISH
Luba tribe, Congo-Kinshasa
Wood, other materials, 5½″ high. 67.116

429   STOOL WITH CARYATID
Luba tribe, Congo-Kinshasa
Wood, 23¼″ high. 58.55

430   BOWSTAND WITH STANDING
FEMALE FIGURE
Luba tribe, Congo-Kinshasa
Wood, 38½″ high. 63.112
Partial gift of The Wunderman Foundation

431   STAFF SURMOUNTED BY STANDING
MALE FIGURE
Bemba tribe, Congo-Kinshasa
Wood, iron, 27″ high. 64.32

432   STANDING MALE FIGURE, ANCESTOR
Buye tribe, Congo-Kinshasa
Wood, 31¼″ high. 61.27

433   STANDING MOTHER AND CHILD FIGURE
Lulua tribe, Congo-Kinshasa
Wood, 9¾″ high. 65.85

434   STANDING MALE FIGURE, FETISH
Songe tribe, Congo-Kinshasa
Wood, other materials, 14″ high. 64.60

435   STOOL
Songe tribe, Congo-Kinshasa
Wood, 19″ high. 69.4

436   MASK
Songe tribe, Congo-Kinshasa
Wood, coloring, 17½″ high. 58.171

433
436
434

437 FEMALE FIGURE, PROBABLY FOR
DIVINATION
Songe tribe, Congo-Kinshasa
Ivory, 4⅛″ high. 57.83

438 DOUBLE FIGURE, MALE AND FEMALE,
FOR DIVINATION
Songe tribe, Congo-Kinshasa
Ivory, 5″ high. 66.86

439 HELMET MASK
Kuba tribes, Congo-Kinshasa
Raffia cloth, cowrie shells, other materials
20½″ high. 58.71

440 GABLED BOX
Kuba tribes, Congo-Kinshasa
Wood, 4⅛″ high. 67.56

441 MASK
Kuba or Lele tribes, Congo-Kinshasa
Wood, other materials, 20¼″ high. 67.42
Gift of Mr. and Mrs. Gustave Schindler

442 SEATED MALE FIGURE
Dengese tribe, Congo-Kinshasa
Wood, 21¾″ high. 66.32

443 STANDING MALE FIGURE
Mbole tribe, Congo-Kinshasa
Wood, coloring, 13″ high. 66.28
Gift of Mr. and Mrs. Raymond Wielgus

444 STANDING MALE FIGURE
Mbole tribe, Congo-Kinshasa
Wood, coloring, 33″ high. 68.21

445   ZOOMORPHIC FIGURE
     Zande tribe, Congo-Kinshasa
     Stone, 6″ high. 65.97

446   MASK
     Lega tribe, Congo-Kinshasa
     Ivory, 7⅛″ high. 62.51

447   MASK
     Lega tribe, Congo-Kinshasa
     Ivory, 8½″ high. 61.285

448   MASK
     Lega tribe, Congo-Kinshasa
     Ivory, 8½″ high. 65.4

449   HEAD
     Lega tribe, Congo-Kinshasa
     Ivory, 8¾″ high. 61.65

450   STANDING MALE FIGURE
     Lega tribe, Congo-Kinshasa
     Ivory, 10½″ high. 67.58
     Gift of Mr. and Mrs. Raymond Wielgus

451   SLIT-DRUM
     Yangere tribe, Central African Republic
     Wood, 8¾″ high. 60.149

The Americas

The Indian art of the Americas had a rich and complex history. It began in the second millennium B.C. and continued until the late second millennium A.D.—well over three thousand years of development and change. During this span, many kinds and varieties of buildings, sculpture, and objects were produced. Their purposes were also many: ceremonial, funerary, personal ornament, daily use.

Man was present in the Americas long before he had the time and the talent to embellish his life, or his death, with luxury goods. Initially he was a big-game hunter, tracking down and killing the giant animals that lived on the grasslands of North America. Subsequently he was forced to supplement his diet with wild plants, which he then learned to cultivate. With the cultivation of plants, settled village life began.

It was upon this village life that the great civilizations of the New World developed. Two areas in particular—Mexico and Peru—achieved a greatness of which the art and architecture still give ample testimony: pyramids, temples, fortresses, irrigation systems, palaces are the visible remains of ancient splendor. To learn their story one must turn to archeology, for the written records of the times are few and largely undeciphered, and native traditions were almost totally destroyed during the years of conquest and colonization by the Europeans. Archeology is slowly piecing together the record. It now tells us that large-scale ceremonial structures, sculpture, and luxury goods were all created much earlier than had previously been believed possible. All these manifestations of a major cultural advance over simple village life were present among the Olmec of Mexico and the Chavin of Peru, whose cultural origins go back to the end of the second millennium B.C. Intellectually complex and artistically inventive, the Olmec and Chavin mark the beginnings of high civilization in the New World.

Bering Straits

Alaska

Canada

United States

Atlantic Ocean

Mexico

Cuba

Hispaniola

Puerto Rico

Pacific Ocean

Guatemala
Honduras
Costa Rica
Panama

Venezuela

Colombia

Ecuador

Peru

Brazil

Bolivia

Argentina

THE AMERICAS

Pre-Columbian Gold

In the history of the discovery and conquest of the New World there is no more meaningful a factor than the search for gold. Columbus set the scene when he announced the discovery of America; he spoke of the incalculable wealth of the new lands, the many mines, the rivers full of precious metals. On his last voyage, begun in 1502, he saw the gold 'eagles' of Veraguas and spent much time searching for the gold from which they were made. The same obsessive search motivated the Europeans who came after him. So single-minded was the hunt that less than fifty years after Columbus set foot on the island of San Salvador, all of the areas of great native wealth had been conquered and thoroughly looted of their precious metals. The search continued for centuries after the Conquest, and whenever ancient tombs were discovered their golden contents were melted down into neat bars. Only of late years have the gold relics of the first Americans finally come to be more desirable in their original form than as bullion. Accordingly, the pre-Columbian gold that is today in museums and private collections is largely of recent discovery. Most of it has been found in burials and consists of personal ornaments. The temple and palace decorations, the enormous ceremonial pieces, the imperial treasures, and the entire gardens of gold and silver that were reported by the early chroniclers of the Conquest are all gone. Of the objects that survive, the largest were made specifically for burials: big funerary masks, vessels and containers, ornaments too large or too awkward to have been worn in life. The rest is finery, luxury objects of a very human sort.

In the New World, gold was first worked in Peru. Delicate, hammered ornaments of gold date back to Chavin times, early in the first millennium B.C. From Peru, gold working is believed to have spread northward through Colombia into Panama and Costa Rica, eventually arriving in Mexico almost two thousand years later. The four important areas of gold work are Peru, Colombia, Panama–Costa Rica, and Mexico, and each has its own stylistic personality. Peru, from early through late times, showed a distinct preference for hammered metals, with smooth, broad surfaces and patterned detail. Colombia produced both hammered and cast forms of considerable refinement, achieved the greatest degree of naturalism, and used human features most consistently. The Panama–Costa Rica area preferred cast objects of the most 'grotesque' outline—animals, birds, and a combination of animal, bird, and human elements in heavier, more massively volumed castings. Mexico, too, cast by preference, although hammering was also done, producing many-detailed, finely scaled pieces of iconographic complexity tied to the involved symbolism of the late period.

The Museum of Primitive Art collection includes all of the areas of pre-Columbian gold. Mexico is the least well represented, simply because the total number of Mexican objects extant is very small. Examples of all the styles from Costa Rica and Panama are present, coming from Línea Vieja, the Diquis Delta, and the Chiriqui, Veraguas, and Coclé areas. Typically they are the eagle, frog, double figure pendant, and elaborate pieces with quartz, ivory, or pyrite inlay. The Colombian styles range from the early through the late period: the big hammered pectorals of Calima style with their close-eyed faces, the Tolima 'knife-shaped' winged figures, the great Sinú bird finials, and the late Tairona pieces of constricted form and careful workmanship. The objects from Peru, larger in scale and made primarily for burial, include a group of late silver vessels, reported to be the contents of a single sumptuous tomb in the area of the great city of Chan Chan.

452 LIP PLUG
     Mexico, Mixteca-Puebla, 1250–1500 A.D.
     Provenience unknown
     Gold, 1¼″ long. 68.69

453 PAIR OF EAR ORNAMENTS
     Mexico, Mixteca-Puebla, 1250–1500 A.D.
     Provenience unknown
     Gold, 2⅜″ high. 67.120

454 EAGLE PENDANT
     Costa Rica, 1000–1500 A.D.
     From Diquis Delta(?)
     Gold, 4½″ high. 61.181

455 PENDANT, FIGURE WITH
     CROCODILE HEAD
     Costa Rica, 1000–1500 A.D.
     From Puerto Gonzalez Viquez
     Gold, pyrite, 6″ high. 63.4

456 EAGLE PENDANT
     Panama, Chiriqui, 1100–1500 A.D.
     Provenience unknown
     Gold, 5⅝″ high. 59.217

457 TWO FROG PENDANTS
     Panama, Veraguas, 1100–1500 A.D.
     Provenience unknown
     Gold, 2¾ and 3″ long. 59.222–.223

458 PENDANT, ANTHROPOMORPHIC FIGURE
     Panama, Veraguas, 1100–1500 A.D.
     Provenience unknown
     Gold, 4¼″ high. 58.283

459 PENDANT, PAIR OF CROCODILES
     Panama, Coclé, 1100–1500 A.D.
     From Sitio Conté area(?)
     Gold, quartz, 1½″ high. 58.186

460 PENDANT, PAIR OF BIRDS
     Panama, Coclé, 1100–1500 A.D.
     From Sitio Conté area(?)
     Gold, quartz, 1¾″ high. 57.32

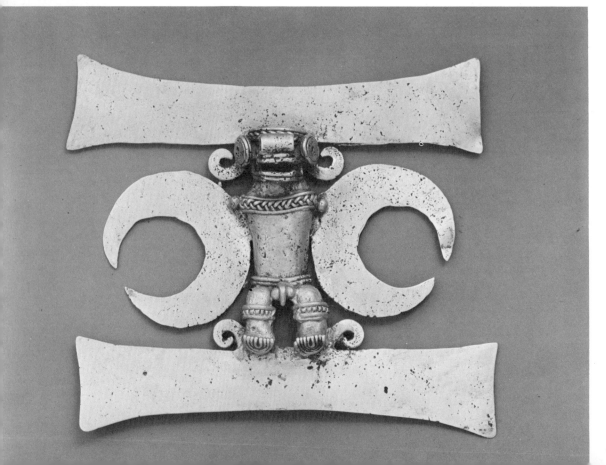

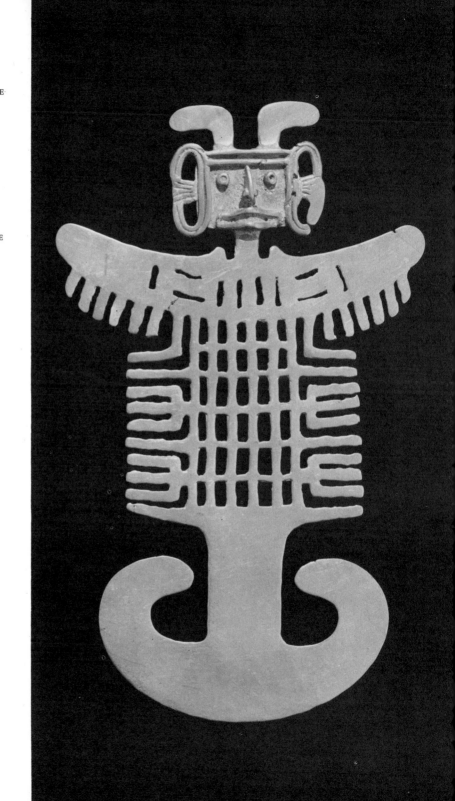

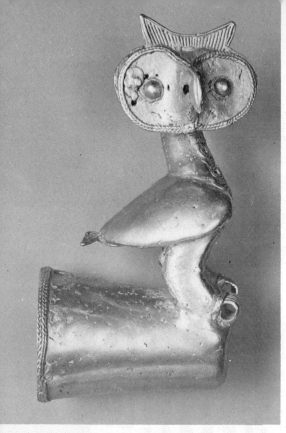

469   PENDANT
Colombia, Chibcha, 1200–1500 A.D.
Provenience unknown
Gold, 4¼″ high. 57.105

470   FUNERARY MASK
Peru, Chimu, 1200–1470 A.D.
North Coast, from Batan Grande
Lambayeque valley
Gold, traces of paint, 28¾″ wide. 57.161

471   GROUP OF SILVER OBJECTS
Peru, Chimu, 1000–1450 A.D.
North Coast, area of Chan Chan
Believed to be the contents of one tomb
Silver, vessel sizes from 5 to 12⅞″ high
65.110, 67.6–.39, 68.73–.74

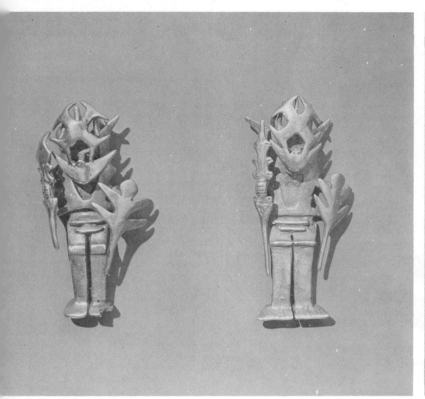

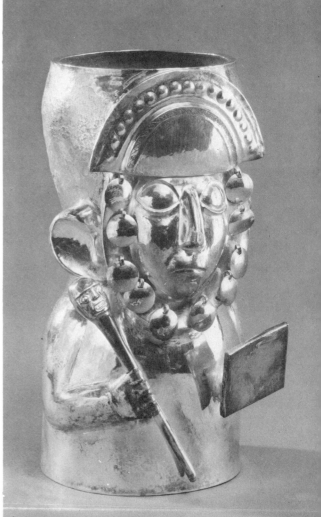

Peru

Except for its narrow, very dry sea coast, Peru is a mountainous country, difficult of access. In pre-Columbian times this small area, tiny in comparison to the rest of South America, produced advanced and organized cultures and built the temples, fortresses, and irrigations systems that mark their greatness.

The first inhabitants of Peru are believed to have been hunters and plant-gatherers. By the beginning of the second millennium B.C. life patterns were established here that were to be characteristically Peruvian, and once pottery was produced—probably by 1800 B.C. and undoubtedly by 1500 B.C.—the stage was set for the great developments.

One of the unusual features of the ancient civilizations of both Peru and Mexico is the grandeur and esthetic greatness of the earliest important cultures. The Chavin of Peru and the Olmec of Mexico were the cultural 'trend-setters' out of which much later culture came, but they also produced works of art that were seldom equaled and, in the minds of some, never surpassed in later times. Chavin art is bold and voluminous, symmetrically balanced, and extremely well made. It appears today as stone sculpture, mostly in the form of architectural decoration, ceramic vessels, gold ornaments, and textiles. Its iconography centers around jaguars, and elements of jaguars combined with human or bird features.

The Chavin heartland was the Maranon River valley in the north central Andes. At one end the river meets the Amazon in the jungles of the Andes' eastern slope (in areas that may have been the source of the Chavin jaguar); at the other end the river reaches almost to the dry valleys of the Pacific coast. From this long highland valley, Chavin influence spread throughout Peru. From north to south the representation of the fanged jaguar indicates Chavin presence.

With the waning of Chavin influence by the mid-first millennium B.C., regional distinctions become pronounced. Paracas and later Nazca in the south coast regions, Mochica in the north, Recuay in the central highlands, are, among others, all stylistically as well as regionally distinct. They do, however, have certain qualities in common—scale (which is moderate), volume (less massive than that of Chavin times), surface decoration (unusually elaborate), and great care of execution and attention to detail. The medium primarily identified with them is pottery, for although gold and wood objects as well as textiles were produced, works of fired clay exist in by far the greatest quantity. The ancient Peruvians had a particular talent for producing what is truly small sculpture in clay, sculpture made with the dual purpose of being useful, functional vessels.

The next major stylistic changes occurred with the rise of the first 'empires' in Peru. By A.D. 600 the Tiahuanaco and Wari empires were developing, the Tiahuanaco in Bolivia and the Wari in the south central highlands of Peru. Although they were separate political entities, it is believed that they shared a common religion—Tiahuanaco in origin—and one result of this was a very similar iconography. Stylistically the art of Tiahuanaco and Wari, and that of the areas which they individually dominated, can be distinguished one from the other, but to do so iconographically is difficult. This is one reason why many objects previously labeled Coast Tiahuanaco, coming from the south coast of Peru, are today known as Wari; it is now realized that they were produced under the sway of the Wari empire. The artistic features common to the two include rectilinear, hieratic images, squareness or straightness

474

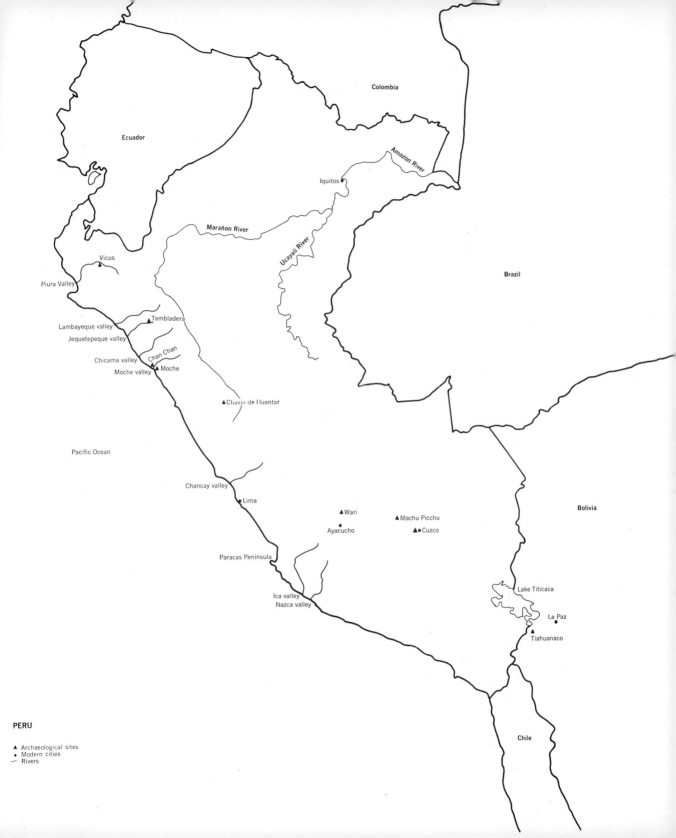

Colombia

Ecuador

Amazon River

Iquitos

Marañon River

Ucayali River

Brazil

Vicus

Piura Valley

Tembladera

Lambayeque valley

Jequetepeque valley

Chicama valley

Chan Chan

Moche valley   Moche

Chavin de Huantar

Pacific Ocean

Chancay valley

Lima

Wari

Ayacucho

Machu Picchu

Cuzco

Bolivia

Paracas Peninsula

Ica valley

Nazca valley

Lake Titicaca

La Paz

Tiahuanaco

Chile

PERU

▲ Archaeological sites
● Modern cities
⌢ Rivers

of form, strongly outlined, and somber colors. The Coast Tiahuanaco styles show their Nazca heritage in being more brightly colored and less rectilinear in outline.

At the disruption of Wari-Tiahuanaco power Peru settled into another period of regionalism, in art styles as in political structures. It was a period of gradual consolidation and growth that culminated in the total domination of Peru by the Inca empire. Artistically it was a period of inattentiveness. Lack of invention and repetition characterize much of the work, although some of it is so inattentive that it achieves spontaneity. This is true, for instance, of many Chancay ceramics and textiles, the latter surviving only because of the extreme dryness of the coastal cemeteries. The textiles are particularly appreciated for their bright colors, simple, large patterns, and seemingly lighthearted subject matter.

The span of the last civilization, the Inca, was short; barely a century before the Spanish conquest had the Inca conquered all of civilized South America. Little Inca art exists today. Following the Conquest the visible Inca objects were disregarded if not destroyed. Those that have survived show a sense of order and balance that is sometimes restrictive, but at best is of classic dimension.

476, 477

472 STIRRUP SPOUT VESSEL
Early Chavin, 1200–1000 B.C.
Provenience unknown
Clay, 9⅛″ high. 58.195

473 STIRRUP SPOUT VESSEL
Early Chavin, 1200–1000 B.C.
Provenience unknown
Clay, 9⅝″ high. 59.4

474 BOTTLE, FELINE HEAD
Late Chavin, 700–500 B.C.
North Coast, from Tembladera
Jequetepeque valley
Clay, resin paint, 12¾″ high. 67.122

475 STIRRUP SPOUT VESSEL
Late Chavin, 700–500 B.C.
North Coast, from Tembladera
Jequetepeque valley
Clay, 11⅜″ high. 68.2

476 BOTTLE, FELINE HEAD
Late Chavin, 700–500 B.C.
North Coast, from Tembladera
Jequetepeque valley
Clay, paint, 8″ high. 68.33

477 STIRRUP SPOUT VESSEL IN FORM OF CAT
Late Chavin, 700–500 B.C.
North Coast, from Tembladera
Jequetepeque valley
Clay, traces of paint, 9⅛″ high. 68.68

478 CUP
Late Chavin, 700–500 B.C.
Provenience unknown
Stone, 3½″ high. 64.9

479

480

481

479 **BRIDGE AND SPOUT VESSEL**
Chavinoid-Paracas, 900–700 B.C.
South Coast, from Juan Pablo, Ica valley
Clay, 8½″ high. 62.121
Gift of Mr. and Mrs. Raymond Wielgus

480 **BRIDGE AND SPOUT VESSEL IN**
FORM OF CAT
Early Paracas, 700–500 B.C.
South Coast, from Callango, Ica valley
Clay, resin paint, 8¼″ long. 65.114

481 **DRUM** (figure is sounding chamber)
Middle Paracas, 500–300 B.C.
South Coast
Clay, resin paint, 15″ high. 63.87

482 **PAINTED TEXTILE**
Middle Paracas, 500–300 B.C.
South Coast, possibly from Ocucaje
Ica valley
Cotton, paint, 21 × 70″. 60.123

483 **BOWL**
Late Paracas, 300–200 B.C.
South Coast
Clay, resin paint, 3⅛″ high. 58.213

484 **WHISTLE IN FORM OF MONKEY**
Late Paracas, 300–200 B.C.
South Coast
Clay, 2″ high. 63.15

485 **DOUBLE SPOUT BOTTLE, TWO FIGURES**
Necropolis, 200–100 B.C.
South Coast
Clay, resin paint, 5″ high. 64.36

486 DOUBLE SPOUT BOTTLE, TROPHY HEAD
Necropolis, 200–100 B.C.
South Coast
Clay, slip, 7¼″ high. 62.166

487 DOUBLE SPOUT BOTTLE
Necropolis, 200–100 B.C.
South Coast
Clay, 6⅜″ high. 60.125

488 VESSEL IN FORM OF SEATED FIGURE
Early Nazca, 100 B.C.—200 A.D.
South Coast
Clay, polychrome slip, 8⅞″ high. 60.67
Gift of Mr. and Mrs. Raymond Wielgus

489 DRUM (figure is sounding chamber)
Early Nazca, 100 B.C.—200 A.D.
South Coast
Clay, polychrome slip, 17¾″ high. 64.4
Gift of Mr. and Mrs. Raymond Wielgus

490 SAMPLER
Early Nazca, 100 B.C.—200 A.D.
South Coast
Wool, cotton, 27¾ × 41¼″. 59.161

491 PAINTED TEXTILE FRAGMENT
Middle Nazca, 200–300 A.D.
South Coast, said to be from Nazca valley
Cotton, paint, 18 × 68½″. 65.112

492 SLEEVELESS SHIRT
Nazca-Wari, 600–700 A.D.
South Coast
Wool, 21 × 26¼″. 58.204

493 MANTLE
Nazca-Wari, 600–700 A.D.
South Coast
Wool, cotton, 128 × 69¾″. 57.262

490 | 497
    | 498

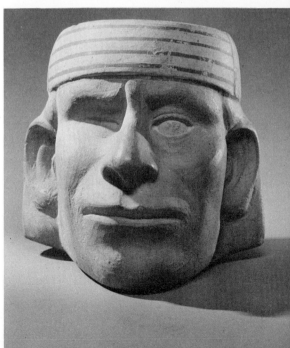

502 VESSEL IN FORM OF HOUSE
Recuay, 300 B.C.—700 A.D.
Central Highlands
Clay, slip, negative decoration, 9¼″ high
68.1

503 SEATED FIGURE
Huaylas, about 700 A.D.
Central Highlands
Stone, 25″ high. 60.102

Middle Period

504 STANDING FIGURE
Tiahuanaco, 300–700 A.D.
Bolivia, Tiahuanaco area
Stone, 18⅜″ high. 59.8

505 VESSEL, STYLIZED PUMA
Tiahuanaco, 300–700 A.D.
Bolivia, Tiahuanaco area
Clay, polychrome slip, 10½″ high. 63.3

506 BOWL
Coast Tiahuanaco (Wari), 600–1000 A.D.
South Coast
Clay, polychrome slip, 3¼″ high. 56.185

507 BOTTLE
Coast Tiahuanaco (Wari), 600–1000 A.D.
South Coast
Clay, polychrome slip, 6″ high. 64.37

508 FRAGMENT OF HEAD VESSEL
Coast Tiahuanaco (Wari), 600–1000 A.D.
South or Central Coast
Clay, slip, 9″ high. 61.14

509 LIME CONTAINER
Coast Tiahuanaco (Wari), 600–1000 A.D.
South Coast, from Coyungo, Nazca valley
Wood, 4½″ high. 65.86

506

507

510

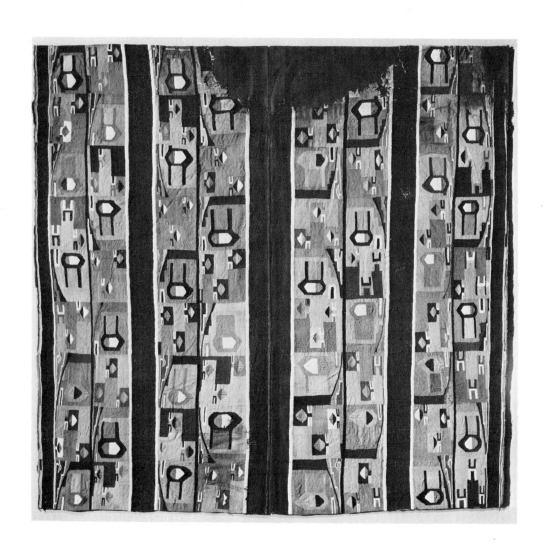

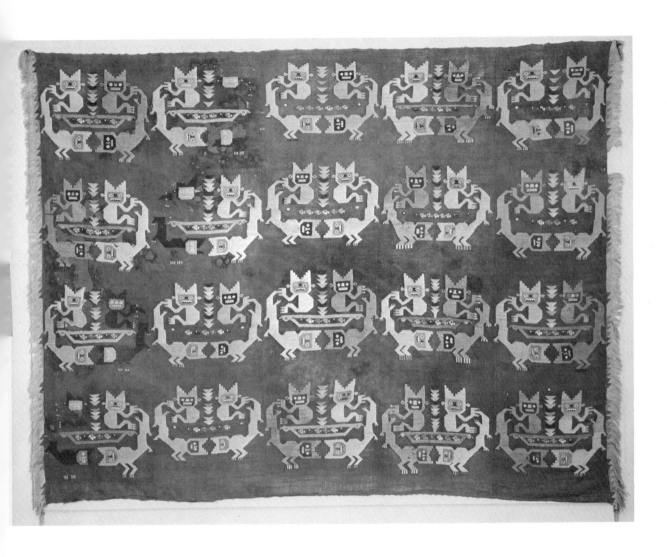

491

510 KERO
Coast Tiahuanaco (Wari), 600–1000 A.D.
South Coast, from Cahuachi, Nazca valley
Wood, 4½″ high. 68.66

511 PAIR OF EAR SPOOLS
Coast Tiahuanaco (Wari), 600–1000 A.D.
South Coast, from Cahuachi, Nazca valley
Bone, shell, stone, 1⅞″ diameter. 68.67

512 MANTLE
Coast Tiahuanaco (Wari), 600–1000 A.D.
South or Central Coast
Wool, cotton, 70×70″. 56.431

513 SLEEVELESS SHIRT
Coast Tiahuanaco (Wari), 600–1000 A.D.
Provenience unknown
Wool, cotton, 41½×42¼″. 56.430

514 WALL HANGINGS
Coast Tiahuanaco (Wari), about 700 A.D.
South Coast, from Hacienda Hispana
Churunga valley
Feathers on cotton fabric, sizes from
26¾×80½″ to 29¼×88⅜″
56.433–.442, 56.444, 57.119, 57.288–.289
58.82–.84, 58.86, 59.195–.196

515 PAINTED HANGING
Coastal Wari, 700–1000 A.D.
Central Coast
Cotton, paint, 33½×147″. 59.278

Late Period

516 TWO SLEEVELESS SHIRTS
Chancay, 1000–1450 A.D.
Central Coast, from Chancay valley(?)
Wool, cotton, 22¼×40″ and 22×39¾″
57.212–.213

517 SHIRT (opened at side seams)
     Chancay, 1000–1450 A.D.
     Central Coast, from Chancay valley(?)
     Wool, cotton, 49⅞× 70″. 61.75

519 SHIRT
     Ica, 1000–1450 A.D.
     South Coast, from Nazca area(?)
     Wool, cotton, 25¾× 59″. 56.432

518 HANGING
     Chancay, 1000–1450 A.D.
     Central Coast, from Chancay valley(?)
     Wool, cotton, 101× 76″. 58.327

520 SHIRT
     Ica, 1000–1450 A.D.
     South Coast
     Wool, cotton, 23½× 30¼″. 57.211

521 PAINTED HANGING
Chimu, 1000–1450 A.D.
North Central Coast
Cotton, paint, 47¾ × 78¼″. 59.239

522 MONKEY EATING FRUIT
Chimu, 1000–1470 A.D.
North Coast, area of Chan Chan(?)
Wood, 14⅝″ high. 56.114

523 STANDING FIGURE
Chimu, 1000–1470 A.D.
North Coast
Wood, 28¼″ high. 58.257

524 SHIRT
Central Coast, 1450–1530 A.D.
Wool, cotton, 18½ × 46¾″. 57.215

525 COSTUME, SHIRT AND LOINCLOTH
Central Coast, 1450–1530 A.D.
Wool, cotton, 19½ × 43½″ and 158 × 45″
57.216

526 COSTUME, LOINCLOTH AND SASH
Central Coast
Wool, cotton, 146 × 44¾″ and 5″ × 15′
57.217

527 ARYBALLUS
Inca, 1438–1532 A.D.
South Highlands, Cuzco area(?)
Clay, slip, 8¼″ high. 61.15

528 ARYBALLUS
Coastal Inca, 1470–1532 A.D.
North Coast, Piura valley
Clay, slip, 7¼″ high. 63.81

532 | 536

The Caribbean

The natives of the Caribbean islands, when Columbus encountered them, were not culturally advanced. Their occupation of the islands is believed to have started shortly before the beginning of the first millennium A.D. when migrations from South America began. They initially came without the knowledge of pottery-making, and much later, in the last few centuries before the Spanish conquest, their greatest achievements both culturally and artistically were made under influences from Mexico. Ceremonial structures and objects then appear. One of the most important of the surviving ceremonial types, an emaciated hunched figure with enormous eyes, is possibly related to the Old Fire God of Mexico.

537 FIGURE OF A GOD OR SPIRIT
Jamaica, about 1500 A.D.
Provenience unknown
Wood, shell inlay, 27″ high. 56.180

538 FIGURE OF A GOD OR SPIRIT
Santo Domingo, date uncertain
From Las Yayas de Viajama, Azua province
Stone, 23″ high. 68.86

539 OBJECT WITH HUMAN FACE
Puerto Rico, Taino, 1300–1400 A.D.
Provenience unknown
Stone, 5½″ high. 57.272

537 | 538

Central America

The isthmus area that connects the two large continents of North and South America includes Panama, Costa Rica, and Nicaragua. They are considered a basic cultural unit, one that was influenced by the greater cultures of Peru to the south and Mexico to the north. The archeology of Nicaragua is little known, while that of Panama and Costa Rica has received considerable attention. Much of this has been occasioned by the gold found in the Panama–Costa Rica area, and by Costa Rica's notable stone sculpture. The small ornamental objects of jade from the Nicoya and Línea Vieja areas, and the large, elaborately carved ceremonial stone pieces from the Highland and Diquis areas, are outstanding. The Highland sculpture in particular is well designed and executed. The subject matter and decorative elements of the larger pieces are rather straightforward human and animal figures, while that of the jades is a more complex mixture.

540 LIDDED VESSEL WITH FANTASTIC
CROCODILE
Costa Rica, about 300 A.D.
Guanacaste province
Clay, 32″ high. 56.178

541 STANDING FIGURE HOLDING
TROPHY HEAD
Costa Rica, about 1000 A.D.
Central Plateau, Reventazón area
Stone, 34¾″ high. 56.279

542 CEREMONIAL METATE
Costa Rica, about 1000 A.D.
Central Plateau, Reventazón area
Stone, 29″ long. 56.290

543 OFFERING TABLE
Costa Rica, about 1000 A.D.
Atlantic watershed area
Stone, 9″ high. 62.103

544 GROUP OF BLUE JADE OBJECTS
Costa Rica, 500–1200 A.D.
Nicoya and Línea Vieja
Jade, from 1⅛ to 5¾″ high
59.41, 59.46, 59.52, 59.58
59.60, 59.62, 65.25, 65.64

545 STYLIZED FIGURE
Costa Rica, 500–1200 A.D.
Línea Vieja, said to be from La Union area
Stone, 4⅛″ high. 66.13

546 STYLIZED TOUCAN
Costa Rica, 500–1200 A.D.
Said to be from Guanacaste province
Stone, 6½″ long. 65.63

547 CEREMONIAL METATE
Honduras, 800–1200 A.D.
Said to be from the Aguán valley
Stone, 39⅜″ long. 59.120

543 | 542

Mexico

Ancient Mexican culture is not, strictly speaking, confined to Mexico. The important areas of indigenous civilization were central-to-south Mexico (the arid north was relatively isolated from the cultural mainstream), Guatemala, British Honduras, and parts of El Salvador and Honduras. So geographically untidy is this spilling over of Mexican culture into different modern countries that the name Mesoamerica has been devised to incorporate them all. This cultural area is divided into two parts—central Mexico, which produced the civilization properly known as Mexican, and the Maya area, extending from southern Mexico south to the limits of Mesoamerica. The Mexican and Maya areas are artistically even more distinct than they are culturally.

Although their remains are meager compared to those of North America proper, big-game hunters were certainly present in central Mexico before 7000 B.C. The vital cultural contribution was made by the hunter-gatherers of the subsequent period, when Mexico played an important role in the domestication of food plants, the most important of which was corn. Corn, originally a highland grass, was the staple food upon which all civilized Indian life in the New World developed. It appeared in domesticated form in the highlands of south-central Mexico by 4000 B.C. and is known to have spread as far south as Peru by 1500 B.C.

The cultural phases of ancient Mexico are defined as preclassic, classic, and postclassic. In the early preclassic period, or between 2000 and 1000 B.C., the Olmecs made their spectacular appearance on the Gulf Coast in the states of Tabasco and Veracruz. With them, ceremonial centers, large stone monuments, and luxury goods entered Mexican culture.

Olmec art exists today in very large-scale to very small-scale stone sculpture, and in ceramic sculpture and vessels. It is fundamentally realistic in form, has solidity and mass, and exhibits considerable refinement of finish. Central to its iconography is an anthropomorphic jaguar, believed to be the earliest form of rain god in Mexico. Olmec remains are found in areas far from the Gulf Coast, but the nature of the contact these remains indicate is unresolved. Olmec influence on both contemporary and later peoples, however, is acknowledged to be extensive.

In the late phases of Olmec art, two major stylistic trends began. Into the Maya area to the south went a trend toward low-relief representational sculpture, with involved, voluted shapes. Into central Mexico, particularly to the Valley of Mexico area, went the solidity, balanced volume, and monumental scale of three-dimensional sculpture. It is the Valley of Mexico and these last artistic characteristics that dominate the subsequent classic period. The great city of Teotihuacan, located not far outside modern Mexico City, was the leading cultural force, and its art had rugged grace and strong angularity. Another important art area during the classic period was central Veracruz, in and around the site of Tajin. It is noted for its elaborately ornamented stone ball-game paraphernalia. The ritual ball game was played from early through late times and was of grave importance. Stone representations of equipment used for the game include objects known as yokes, palmas, and hachas. Those of classic-period Veracruz are richly decorated with volutes and include human and animal figures and motifs. During both the preclassic and classic periods central Veracruz also produced an important amount of clay sculpture, some of which reached amazingly large size.

The classic period ended at different times in different parts of Mexico. Teotihuacan was the first center to succumb, the city destroyed by invaders about A.D. 650. In other areas the period lasted until A.D. 900, at which time the postclassic is considered to begin. The postclassic was a period of great change. Ancient patterns were altered, new ideologies evolved. The most outwardly meaningful change was a new aggressiveness, manifest in highly developed military states.

The art of the postclassic period is elegant, varied, and technically excellent. All available materials and possible techniques were employed to produce a wide range of luxury goods and ceremonial objects. Gold (which appears only now—late—in Mexico), jade, bone, shell, feathers— all can be found in delicately wrought yet highly dramatic personal ornaments. Unusually thin, colorfully surfaced pottery of functional shape was used, at least by the Aztec nobility. Ceremonial objects of stone attained great size. The complex iconography of the period is part of a religious symbolism that allowed for the assimilation of gods and their attributes from earlier, neighboring, and conquered peoples. The intellectual bias of the militarily oriented societies produced an art of extraordinary austerity and power in which ideas of death were frequently present. Such was Aztec art when it was first seen by Europeans in the early sixteenth century.

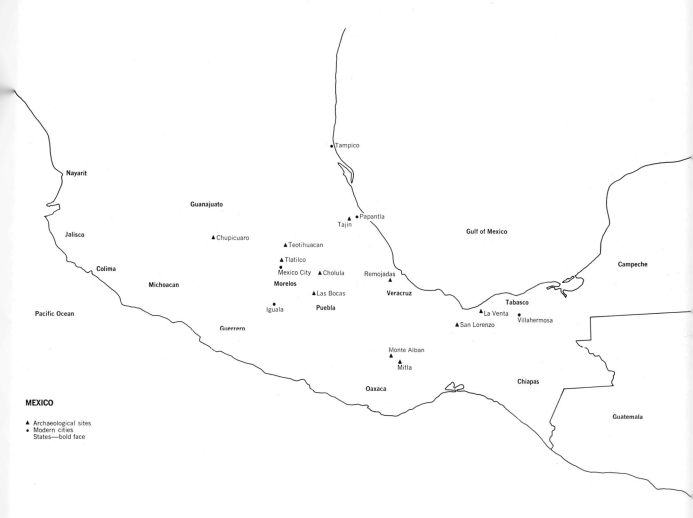

Tampico •

Papantla •
▲
Tajin

Nayarit

Guanajuato

Gulf of Mexico

Campeche

Jalisco

▲ Chupicuaro

▲ Teotihuacan

Colima

▲ Tlatilco
• Mexico City
Morelos

▲ Cholula

Remojadas
▲

Veracruz

Tabasco

▲ Las Bocas
Michoacan

• Iguala
Puebla

La Venta
▲
• Villahermosa

Pacific Ocean

Guerrero

▲ San Lorenzo

Monte Alban
▲
▲ Mitla

Chiapas

Oaxaca

Guatemala

MEXICO

▲ Archaeological sites
• Modern cities
States—bold face

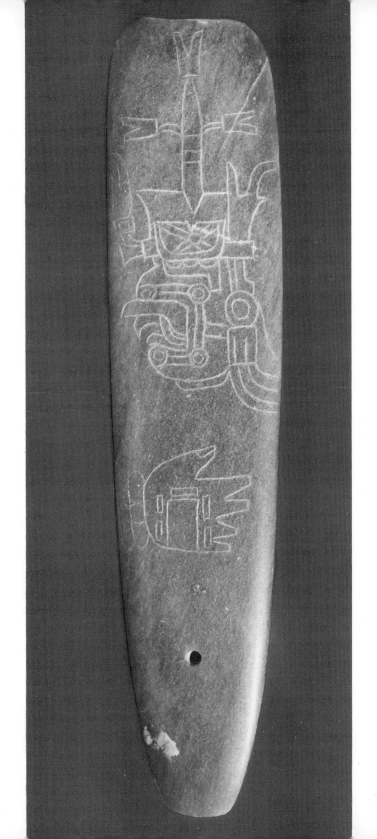

555 INCISED CELT
Olmec, 1200–400 B.C.
Provenience unknown
Jade, 14⅜″ high. 56.52

556 PECTORAL
Olmec, 1200–400 B.C.
Provenience unknown
Jade, 4¼″ wide. 60.152

557 CEREMONIAL OBJECT ('spoon')
Olmec, 1200–400 B.C.
Guerrero
Jade, 6⅝″ long. 65.107

558 SEATED FIGURE
Olmec, 1200–400 B.C.
From Las Bocas, Puebla
Clay, red pigment, 13⅜″ high. 65.28

559 BOTTLE
Olmec, 1200–400 B.C.
From Las Bocas, Puebla
Clay, red pigment, 7¾″ high. 63.48

560 BOWL
Olmec, 1200–400 B.C.
From San Martin Texmelucan, Puebla
Clay, traces of pigment, 4½″ high. 56.157

561 SMALL YOKE
Olmec, 800–400 B.C.
Said to be from Guerrero
Stone, 7½″ high. 58.200

562 SMALL YOKE
Olmec, 800–400 B.C.
Tlatilco, Valley of Mexico
Stone, 5⅜″ high. 64.35

558 | 561
562

563 MASK
Tlatilco, 900–300 B.C.
Valley of Mexico
Clay, pigment, 5¼″ high. 63.31

564 GROUP OF FIGURES
Tlatilco, 900–300 B.C.
Valley of Mexico
Clay, pigments, from 2⅞ to 5⅝″ high. 61.151
61.153, 61.155–.157, 61.163

565 GROUP OF FIGURES
Chupicuaro, 300–100 B.C.
Guanajuato
Clay, pigments, from 1¾ to 4¼″ high
59.78, 61.129, 61.131–.132
61.143–.144, 61.147–.148

566 VESSEL, FIGURE SEATED ON STOOL
Central Highlands, 900–300 B.C.
Possibly from Tlatilco
Clay, 13¾″ high. 65.142

567 MONKEY HEAD JAR
Monte Alban I(?), 800–300 B.C.
Oaxaca
Clay, 8½″ high. 57.199

568 VESSEL WITH EFFIGY FIGURE
Monte Alban II, 300–100 B.C.
Oaxaca
Clay, 7⅞″ high. 61.32

569 STANDING FIGURE
Mezcala, 300 B.C.—300 A.D.
Guerrero
Stone, 6½″ high. 69.10

564, 564, 564 | 572
| 573

570 STANDING FIGURE
Mezcala, 300 B.C.—300 A.D.
Guerrero
Stone, 13¾″ high. 59.266
Gift of Luis de Hoyos

571 STANDING FIGURE
Mezcala, 300 B.C.—300 A.D.
Guerrero
Stone, 4″ high. 68.47

572 MASK
Mezcala, 300 B.C.—300 A.D.
Guerrero
Stone, 5½″ high. 57.137

573 TEMPLE, WITH RECLINING FIGURE
Mezcala, 300 B.C.—300 A.D.
Guerrero
Stone, 7⅛″ high. 57.104

Classic Period

574 STANDING FIGURE
Teotihuacan, 200–600 A.D.
Provenience unknown
Stone, 16⅛″ high. 57.201

575 MASK
Teotihuacan, 200–600 A.D.
Provenience unknown
Stone, 9⅜″ high. 57.117

576 MASK
Teotihuacan, 200–600 A.D.
Guerrero
Onyx, 7½″ high. 67.118

574 | 575

577 SEATED FIGURE
Teotihuacan, 200–600 A.D.
Provenience unknown
Stone, 1⅞″ high. 58.48

578 TRIPOD BOWL
Teotihuacan, 200–600 A.D.
Valley of Mexico
Clay, 9¾″ high. 56.154

579 YOKE
Classic Veracruz, 300–900 A.D.
Veracruz, said to be from Papantla area
Stone, 15¾″ long. 56.280

580 YOKE
Classic Veracruz, 300–900 A.D.
Veracruz, said to be from Papantla area
Stone, 17⅜″ long. 56.281

581 CLOSED YOKE
Classic Veracruz, 300–900 A.D.
Veracruz
Stone, 18⅞″ long. 56.336

582 PALMA
Classic Veracruz, 300–900 A.D.
Veracruz, said to be from Nautla area
Stone, 18⅛″ high. 56.283

583 PALMA
Classic Veracruz, 300–900 A.D.
Veracruz, said to be from Nautla area
Stone, 20⅛″ high. 56.284

584 HACHA IN FORM OF FISH
Classic Veracruz, 300–900 A.D.
Veracruz, Ignacio de la Llave(?)
Stone, shell inlays, paint, 14⅞″ high. 66.12

585 HACHA, HEAD IN JAGUAR MASK
Classic Veracruz, 300–900 A.D.
Veracruz
Stone, 8¾" high. 56.163

586 HACHA, HANDS
Classic Veracruz, 300–900 A.D.
Veracruz
Stone, 7" high. 62.48

587 WHISTLE, STANDING FIGURE
WITH BIRD HEAD
Classic Veracruz, 300–900 A.D.
Veracruz
Clay, 20¼" high. 61.73

588 HOWLING COYOTE
Remojadas, 300–900 A.D.
Veracruz
Clay, paint, 20" high. 60.185

589 SEATED FEMALE FIGURE
Remojadas, 300–900 A.D.
Veracruz
Clay, 33⅛" high. 61.23

590 HALF FIGURE OF EHECATL (God of wind)
Remojadas(?), 300–900 A.D.
Veracruz, said to be from San Andres Tuxtla
Clay, 33¾" high. 57.132

591 VESSEL IN FORM OF BOUND PRISONER
Colima, 300–600 A.D.
State of Colima
Clay, 21" high. 57.3

592 VESSEL IN FORM OF WARRIOR
Colima, 300–600 A.D.
State of Colima
Clay, 14⅜" high. 57.9

593 VESSEL·IN FORM OF CRAYFISH
Colima, 300–600 A.D.
State of Colima
Clay, 13½″ long. 68.61

594 PAIR OF SEATED FIGURES
Nayarit, 300–600 A.D.
State of Nayarit
Clay, slip, 16¼″ high. 66.47

595 KNEELING FEMALE FIGURE
Nayarit (Chinesco), 300–600 A.D.
State of Nayarit
Clay, slip, 11″ high. 63.65

596 VESSEL, FIGURE WITH HEAD .ON ARMS
Nayarit, 300–600 A.D.
State of Nayarit
Clay, slip, 7⅝″ high. 63.88

Post-Classic Period

597 TLALOC MASK (God of rain)
Mixteca-Puebla, 1250–1500 A.D.
Provenience unknown
Stone, 5½″ high. 62.169

598 PENDANT FIGURE
Mixteca-Puebla, 1250–1500 A.D.
Provenience unknown
Stone, 2⅝″ high. 62.21

599 PLAQUE
Mixteca-Puebla, 1250–1500 A.D.
Said to have been found in Guerrero
Stone, 5½″ long. 64.38

600 PART OF THROWING STICK(?)
Mixteca-Puebla, 1250–1500 A.D.
Oaxaca
Antler, 5″ high. 57.89

601 COLLAR-BASE BOWL
Mixteca-Puebla, 1250–1500 A.D.
Puebla, possibly from Cholula
Clay, polychrome slip, 4⅝″ high. 56.155

602 MACUILXOCHITL (God of flowers
music, and dance)
Mixteca-Puebla, 1250–1500 A.D.
Oaxaca, said to come from Teotitlan
del Camino
Clay, paint, 22⅝″ high. 56.160

603 MACUILXOCHITL HEAD (God of flowers
Music, and dance)
Mixteca-Puebla, 1250–1500 A.D.
Oaxaca
Clay, paint, 7½″ high. 56.158

604 EFFIGY VESSEL, POSSIBLY EHECATL
(God of wind)
Mixteca-Puebla(?), 1250–1500 A.D.
Provenience unknown
Onyx, 9¼″ high. 61.33

605 EFFIGY VESSEL, MONKEY
HOLDING ITS TAIL
Mixteca-Puebla(?), 1250–1500 A.D.
Said to have been found in Michoacan
Onyx, inlays, 7½″ high. 66.1

606 FIGURE OF MAN LEANING ON STAFF
Huastec, 900–1200 A.D.
Northern Veracruz
Stone, 34⅜″ high. 56.291

607 HEAD (from a figure)
Huastec, 900–1200 A.D.
Northern Veracruz
Stone, 8″ high. 58.46

594 | 597
| 598, 599

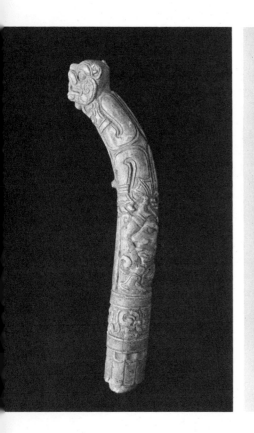

608 VESSEL IN FORM OF SEATED FIGURE
Huastec, 1400–1500 A.D.
Northern Veracruz
Clay, paint, 13½″ high. 65.75

609 BOWL, VULTURE WITH MOVABLE HEAD
Isla de Sacrificios, 1400–1500 A.D.
Central Veracruz, from Boca del Rio
Clay, slip, 12¾″ long. 61.105

610 RATTLESNAKE
Aztec, 1300–1520 A.D.
Valley of Mexico(?)
Stone, 14″ high. 57.2

611 QUETZALCOATL
Aztec, 1300–1520 A.D.
Valley of Mexico(?)
Stone, 22½″ high. 57.242

612 XIPE TOTEC (God of growth
and rejuvenation)
Aztec, 1300–1520 A.D.
Said to have been found in Puebla
Clay, 56¾″ high. 63.162

613 TRIPOD VESSEL
Aztec, 1327–1481 A.D.
Valley of Mexico(?)
Clay, 14⅛″ high. 56.150

604, 605 | 606

Maya Area

Maya art is one of the great American contributions to the art of the world. Its diversity of form and variety of style, its individuality and sophistication of image make it unique in the New World. Mexican art, by contrast, is solid, strong, and traditional; Maya art is fluid, graceful, and spontaneous. It could be called the most beautiful that ancient America produced. The most important period in this art is the classic, from A.D. 300 to 900, corresponding to the same period in Mexican culture. The Maya of preclassic times are imperfectly known, and by the postclassic period warrior peoples from central Mexico dominated Yucatan, the last focus of Maya culture.

Maya art divides into three distinct style areas: the southern, located in the highlands of the Pacific coast; the central, in the rain forests of northern Guatemala; and the northern, in the Mexican states at the top of the Yucatan peninsula. It was the central area that produced the mightiest of classic-period centers and the art that is most frequently taken to exemplify the Maya style.

The Maya are known for their sculpture, architecture, painting, and a multitude of minor arts—personal luxury objects of jade and shell, ritual and burial pieces of obsidian and flint, ceramic forms in great variety. Free-standing sculpture, the commemorative stones known as steles and their associated altars, and the architecture of the great ceremonial centers are the most spectacular of Maya forms. Since there is rather little organization of interior or exterior space, this architecture may perhaps be considered as enormously large-scale sculpture. It is characterized by its mass, by the formal relationships of one structure to another, and by its ornate exterior decoration of façades, walls, roof combs, staircases, and courtyards. Within the main ceremonial areas, among the pyramids, temples, and palaces, were set the sculptured altars and steles. The steles, large rectangular stones, are carved, usually in low relief, on from one to four sides. They were erected to record important events or to mark important calendar days, time calculations being a principal Maya interest.

Another, more unusual, place for low-relief commemorative panels was on the lintels of temple or palace doorways. The walls of these structures were so massive that some of the lintels attain a depth of seven feet. Some of the few wood lintels that have survived, as well as some of the many carved in stone, have retained enough trace of paint to recall their original bright polychrome surface.

Notable among the Maya ceramics are the hollow figurines found in burials on the island of Jaina off the Campeche coast. These figures, many of which were painted, usually represent a warrior, priest, or ball player.

The bright polychrome ceramic vessels of the Maya are particularly interesting in that the spontaneous brushwork on their surfaces is perhaps the principal surviving instance of Maya painting. Only a small number of wall paintings are known, but on vessel as on wall the painting of the Maya is two-dimensional, space-filling, linear work of much sureness and subtlety.

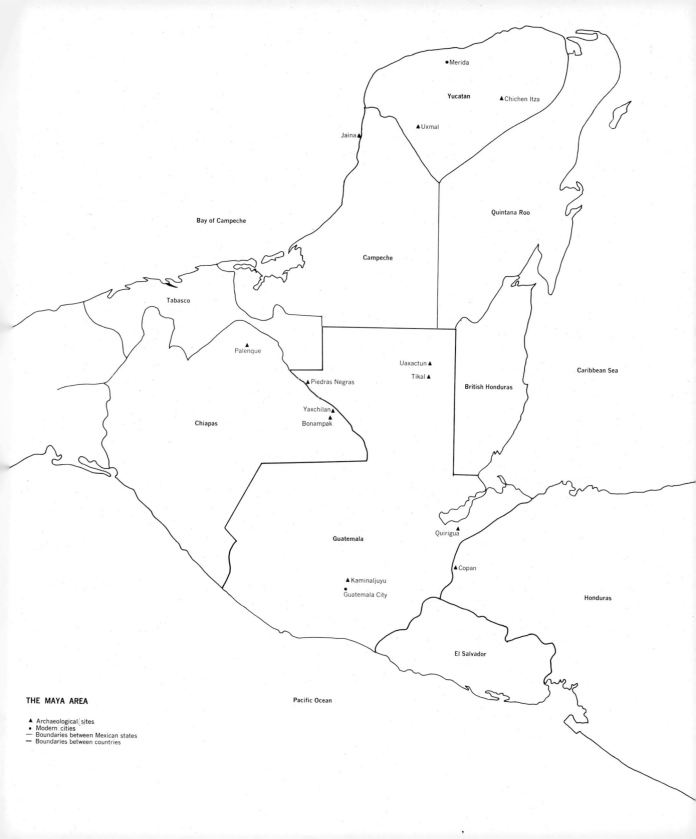

Merida

Yucatan

▲Chichen Itza

▲Uxmal

Jaina▲

Bay of Campeche

Quintana Roo

Campeche

Tabasco

Palenque ▲

▲Piedras Negras

Uaxactun ▲

Tikal ▲

British Honduras

Caribbean Sea

Chiapas

Yaxchilan▲
▲
Bonampak

Quirigua ▲

Guatemala

▲Copan

Kaminaljuyu ▲
•
Guatemala City

Honduras

El Salvador

Pacific Ocean

THE MAYA AREA

▲ Archaeological sites
• Modern cities
— Boundaries between Mexican states
— Boundaries between countries

614 KNEELING FIGURE OF DIGNITARY
     OR PRIEST
     Early Classic Maya, about 500 A.D.
     Mexico, said to have been found near
     Tabasco-Guatemala border
     Wood, 14″ high. 62.172

615 DOUBLE-CHAMBERED VESSEL
     Early Classic Maya, 300–600 A.D.
     Mexico or possibly the Peten area
     Clay, 11⅞″ high. 62.46

616 CYLINDRICAL JAR, MYTHOLOGICAL
     SCENE
     Late Classic Maya, 600–900 A.D.
     Mexico
     Clay, slip, 5½″ high. 68.7

617 CYLINDRICAL VESSEL, TWO
     DIGNITARIES
     Late Classic Maya, 600–900 A.D.
     Mexico
     Clay, polychrome slip, 6⅝″ high. 67.121

618 CYLINDRICAL JAR, ENTHRONED
     FIGURES
     Late Classic Maya, 600–900 A.D.
     Guatemala, said to be from Nebaj area
     Clay, polychrome slip, 8⅜″ high. 67.1
     Gift of Mrs. Gertrud A. Mellon

619 CYLINDRICAL VESSEL, BIRD-HEADED
     FIGURES
     Late Classic Maya, 600–900 A.D.
     Guatemala
     Clay, polychrome slip, 7¾″ high. 64.15

620 BOWL
     Late Classic Maya, 600–900 A.D.
     Mexico, Yucatan
     Clay, 4½″ high. 62.105

615 | 617
    | 618

621 TRIPOD PLATE, DANCING FIGURE
Late Classic Maya, 600–900 A.D.
Mexico, Campeche
Clay, polychrome slip, 11⅝" diameter. 64.33

622 WHISTLE IN FORM OF THE FAT GOD
Late Classic Maya, 600–900 A.D.
Mexico, said to be from Uaymil Island
Campeche
Clay, paint, 11½" high. 61.72

623 FIGURE WITH REMOVABLE HELMET MASK
Late Classic Maya, 600–900 A.D.
Mexico, from Jaina Island, Campeche
Clay, 6⅝" high. 65.116

624 URN, FIGURE STANDING ON TURTLE
Late Classic Maya, 600–900 A.D.
Mexico, Chiapas
Clay, traces of paint, 21¼" high. 63.1
Gift of Mr. and Mrs. Raymond Wielgus

625 LINTEL, PRESENTATION SCENE
Late Classic Maya, 600–900 A.D.
Mexico, Yaxchilan-Bonampak area
Chiapas
Stone, paint, 35" high. 62.102

626 COLUMN
Late Classic Maya, 600–900 A.D.
Mexico, Campeche(?)
Stone, 68⅝" high. 62.3

627 STELA
Late Classic Maya, 600–900 A.D.
Guatemala, from Piedras Negras
Stone, 96" high. 63.163

628 ORNAMENTS
Late Classic Maya, 600–900 A.D.
Provenience unknown
Shell, 2½ and 3¾″ high. 63.18, 61.69
Gift of Mrs. Gertrud A. Mellon: 63.18

629 ORNAMENT
Pre-Classic Maya, 300 B.C.—300 A.D.
Guatemala, from Kaminaljuyu
Jade, 3½″ long. 60.153
Gift of Mr. and Mrs. Julius Carlebach

630 CROSS-LEGGED FIGURE
Early Classic Maya, 300–600 A.D.
Honduras, from Copan area
Jade, 4¼″ high. 63.21

631 SCEPTER, HEADDRESSED FIGURE
WITH SMALLER FIGURE ON BACK
Late Classic Maya, 600–900 A.D.
Guatemala, Peten area
Eccentric flint, 13⅝″ high. 67.63

632 HEAD OF CHAC (God of rain)
Maya-Toltec, 900–1000 A.D.
Mexico, from Chichen Itza, Yucatan
Stone, 13¾″ high. 57.66

North America

North America never attained the cultural importance of its southern neighbors. Much impetus came from Mexico, as in the Southwest—the only North American area in which a cultural tradition can be traced continuously from its remote beginnings into historic times. Here corn cultivation and pottery making—the two vital components of New World civilization—originated under Mexican influence. Much later, in the Mississippian tradition of the Southeast, specific formal and iconographic similarities to Mesoamerican art can be found.

Arctic North America was inhabited by a people racially and linguistically different from the American Indian, the Eskimo, who developed a hunting culture specifically adapted to the conditions of the northern climate. Eskimo art, produced in its most characteristic and continuous form in northern Alaska, appeared about 300 B.C., with ivory hunting implements and tools (now beautifully patined), and lasted, with considerable changes, until the early twentieth century.

The Indian of North America, because of his great cultural diversity and lack of a centralized civilization such as existed in Mexico and Peru, maintained himself longer in the face of the European onslaught. From the sixteenth century on he was gradually pushed from his lands, and in the 1880s, when there was no further place for him to go, he was finally isolated onto reservations. During this period of increasing confinement at least two vigorous artistic traditions flourished, reaching their peak in the nineteenth century: the art of the Northwest Coast Indians and that of the Plains Indians, the latter the redskin *par excellence* of movie and television.

The basic medium of Northwest Coast art is wood, and it was the increased availability of metal tools and income from the fur trade that accounted for much of its dynamic development in the first half of the nineteenth century. This is an art of formal precision, symbolic design, and strong color. It appears in totem poles, house posts, and mural paintings, all of monumental character, and in household utensils, fishing implements, personal ornaments, ceremonial costumes, masks, and dance accessories.

The culture of the Plains Indians, which so appeals to the romantic imagination, was totally dependent upon the horse, an animal introduced to the New World by the Spanish. The art of these Indians, particularly painting in its later forms, is perhaps the most acculturated to be found on the continent. Their pictorial tradition for recounting heroic exploits in the life of a warrior or chief was transformed, for a very brief period, into the glorification of Plains Indian life and values. Simple outline drawings (many made with stencils), bright flat colors, and traditional symbols were put down on animal hides, fabric, and paper, with Indian, white man, and horse presented in an idiom clearly influenced by white imagery and taste. These drawings are pictorially unsophisticated and 'charmingly' naïve, yet they are beautiful and vital statements about a way of life that was dying even as the works of art were being produced.

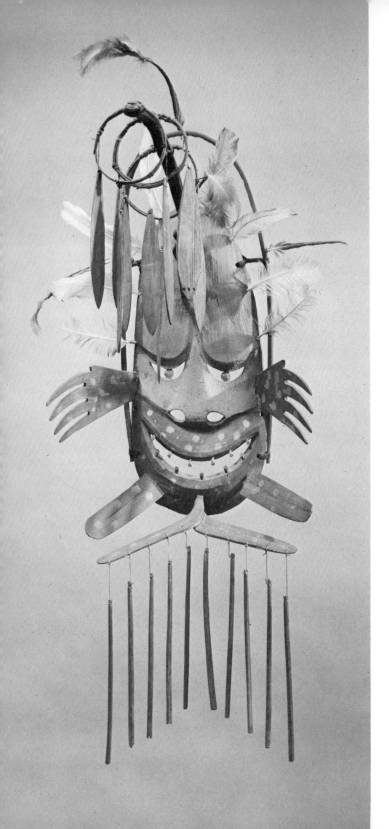

633 GROUP OF IVORY OBJECTS
Eskimo, 100 B.C.—700 A.D.
Alaska
Ivory, from 3¼ to 7⅞″ long
57.273, 58.5, 61.241, 64.54–.57
Gift of Mr. and Mrs. Raymond
Wielgus: 61.241

634 MASK
Eskimo, late 19th century
Alaska, Kuskokwim River
Wood, paint, feathers, string, 45¼″ high
61.39

635 MASK
Eskimo, late 19th century
Alaska, Kuskokwim River
Wood, paint, 19⅜″ high. 61.40

636 MASK
Eskimo, 19th century(?)
Alaska
Wood, paint, feathers, rawhide, 24″ high
63.167

637 CLUB
British Columbia, date uncertain
Area of Skeena River
Stone, 14½″ long. 64.81

638 STANDING FEMALE FIGURE
Kwakiutl, 19th century(?)
British Columbia
Wood, 50″ high. 56.205

639 HEADDRESS ORNAMENT
Tsimshian(?), 19th century
British Columbia
Wood, paint, shell inlays, 7⅞″ high. 56.333

640 HEADDRESS ORNAMENT
Style undetermined, late 19th century
Alaska or British Columbia
Wood, paint, shell inlays, 7¼" high. 57.277

641 RATTLE IN FORM OF CRANE
Style undetermined, late 19th century
Alaska or British Columbia
Wood, ivory, 8¾" high. 56.334

642 RATTLE
Tsimshian, late 19th century
British Columbia
Wood, leather, 12⅝" high
62.152

643 CEREMONIAL COPPER
Tlingit, late 19th century
Alaska
Copper, 34¼" high. 65.104

644 FIGHTING KNIFE
Tlingit, late 19th century
Alaska
Ivory, iron, shell inlays, leather, 14⅝" high
59.103

645 DEAD-MAN MASK
Tlingit, 19th century(?)
Alaska
Wood, paint, hide, metal, 13⅝" high. 56.330

646 SEA-BEAR MASK
Haida or Tlingit, late 19th century
British Columbia or Alaska
Copper, fur, shell inlays, 12" high. 58.329

647 PAIR OF PADDLES
   Haida, late 19th century
   British Columbia
   Wood, paint, 56″ long. 66.58

649 'SLAVE-KILLER'
   California, date uncertain
   Provenience unknown
   Stone, 13⅜″ long. 59.214

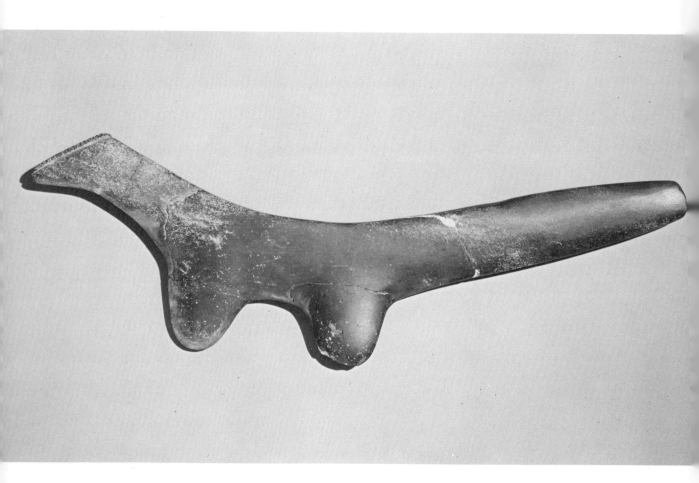

648 'SLAVE-KILLER'
   Columbia River, date uncertain
   Oregon, found near Sauvies Island
   Stone, 14¼″ long. 58.229

650 THREE FIGURES
   Columbia River, mid-18th century
   Oregon, area of the Dalles
   Bone, 6¾ to 7″ high. 68.82–.84
   Gift of Mr. and Mrs. Robert W. Campbell

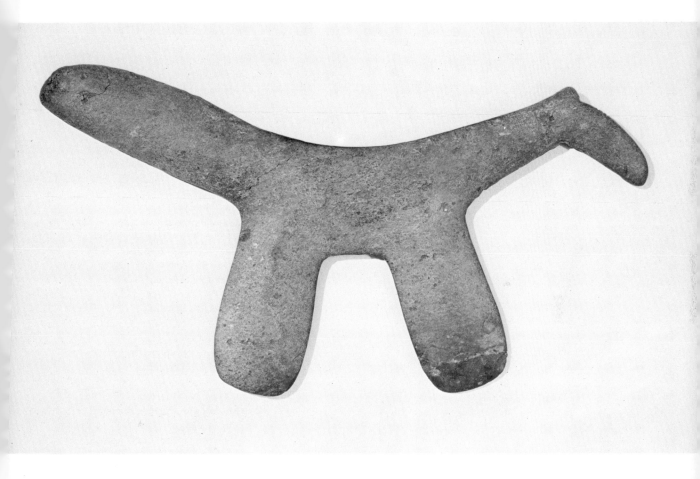

651 ARROW SHAFT STRAIGHTENER
Columbia River, 14th century
Oregon, area of the Dalles
Stone, 5¼″ long. 68.85
Gift of Mr. and Mrs. Robert W. Campbell

652 PIPE OR SMOKE BLOWER IN
FORM OF WHALE
Cañalino, about 1000 A.D.
California, from Arroyo Sequit Canyon(?)
Los Angeles County
Stone, shell inlays, 16½″ long. 57.134

653 'PELICAN STONE'
Cañalino, about 1000 A.D.
California, Los Angeles County(?)
Stone, shell and pearl inlays, 4¾″ high
58.216

654 TWO WHISTLES AND FLUTE
Cañalino, about 1000 A.D.
California, from Arroyo Sequit
Canyon(?), Los Angeles County
Bone, shell and quartz inlay in asphalt
9¾ to 13″ high. 56.201–.203

655 KNEELING FIGURE
Mississippian (Temple Mound II period)
1200–1600 A.D.
Tennessee, from the Duck River
Stone, 26¼″ high. 57.1

656 HEAD (from a figure)
Mississippian (Temple Mound II period)
1200–1600 A.D.
Tennessee, found near Clarksville
Stone, 7½″ high. 65.68

657 PENDANT WITH RATTLESNAKE DESIGN
Mississippian (Temple Mound II period)
1200–1600 A.D.
Tennessee, from Chickamuaga Creek
Shell, 4¼″ high. 56.389

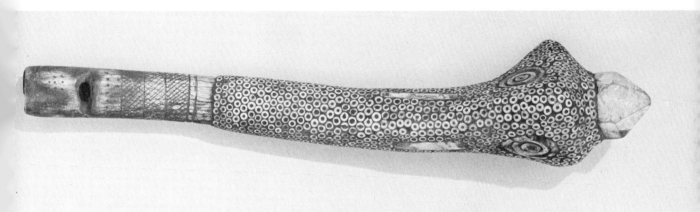

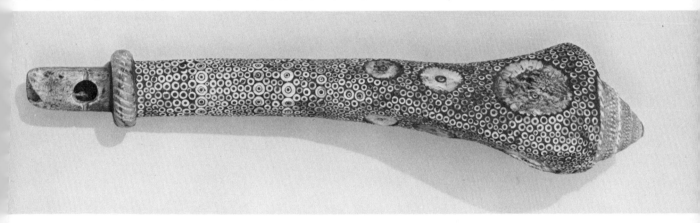

650, 650 | 654

654

658 MASKS
Mississippian (Temple Mound II period)
1200–1600 A.D.
Tennessee, from Williams Island
Shell, 6⅜ and 6¾″ high. 58.77–.78

659 BOTTLE
Caddoan, 1200–1600 A.D.
Arkansas, from Yell County
Clay, 8¾″ high. 61.244
Gift of Mr. and Mrs. Raymond Wielgus

660 SKETCHBOOK (88 drawings)
Cheyenne and Arapaho, dated 1884
Oklahoma, made on Darlington
Agency reservation
Watercolor, ink, colored and lead
pencil on paper
Page size 11¾ × 5¼″. 68.12

661 BUFFALO ROBE WITH WOMAN'S DESIGN
Arapaho, 19th century
Wyoming
Hide, paint, 73 × 80″. 64.50

662 WAR GOD
Pueblo, 19th–20th century
New Mexico, Zuñi
Wood, traces of paint, 29¾″ high. 64.8
Gift of Mr. and Mrs. Raymond Wielgus

663 KACHINA MASK
Pueblo, 20th century
New Mexico, Zuñi
Hide, paint, feathers, cotton, 9⅝″ high. 64.2

664 KACHINA MASK
Pueblo, 20th century
New Mexico, Santo Domingo or Cochiti
Hide, wood, paint, feathers, gourd
13¼″ high. 64.1

T